Essential
ChromeBook

Kevin Wilson

www.elluminetpress.com

Essential ChromeBook

Publisher: Elluminet Press
Director: Kevin Wilson
Lead Editor: Steven Ashmore
Technical Reviewer: Mike Taylor, Robert Ashcroft
Copy Editors: Joanne Taylor, James Marsh
Proof Reader: Mike Taylor
Indexer: James Marsh
Cover Designer: Kevin Wilson

eBook versions and licenses are also available for most titles. Any source code or other supplementary materials referenced by the author in this text is available to readers at

www.elluminetpress.com/resources

For detailed information about how to locate your book's resources, go to

www.elluminetpress.com/resources

Table of Contents

About the Author

Kevin Wilson has made a career out of technology and showing others how to use it. After earning a master's degree in computer science, software engineering, and multimedia systems, Kevin worked as a tutor and college instructor, helping students master such subjects as multimedia, computer literacy and information technology. He currently serves as Elluminet Press Publishing's senior writer and director, he periodically teaches computing at college in South Africa and serves as an IT trainer in England.

Kevin's motto is clear: "If you can't explain something simply, you haven't understood it well enough." To that end, he has created the Computer Essentials series, in which he breaks down complex technological subjects into smaller, easy-to-follow steps that students and ordinary computer users can put into practice.

Acknowledgements

Thanks to all the staff at Luminescent Media & Elluminet Press for their passion, dedication and hard work in the preparation and production of this book.

To all my friends and family for their continued support and encouragement in all my writing projects.

To all my colleagues, students and testers who took the time to test procedures and offer feedback on the book

Finally thanks to you the reader for choosing this book. I hope it helps you to use your computer with greater ease.

What is a ChromeBook?

A ChromeBook is a laptop or a tablet that runs an operating system called Chrome OS which is designed by Google around the Google Chrome web browser and is designed to work almost completely online.

It's worth noting what a ChromeBook can do and what it can't do. ChromeBooks are great for online collaboration - creating and sharing documents and presentations with google docs, using the web, checking your email/social media, posting photographs and videos, video chatting with friends as well as streaming music, TV programmes and films directly to your ChromeBook.

A ChromeBook on the other hand would be a bad choice if you needed a laptop/device to edit video, make music, manipulate photographs, anything that requires a lot of data storage and processing speed, or play the latest computer games. ChromeBooks are not designed for this.

Chapter 1: What is a ChromeBook?

ChromeBooks are designed to be always connected to the internet, meaning you always need an internet connection whether you are at home, the office, in school, college, the library or generally out and about. This could be through your home cable/broadband internet provider, work/college network, 4G cell connection or WiFi hotspot. Without an internet connection, your ChromeBook will be useless or very limited at best.

As you can see from the photograph below, ChromeBooks look very similar to traditional style windows or mac laptops. The main difference is ChromeBooks are a lot more light weight, usually smaller, have less built in storage space and have no DVD/CD drives.

Let's take a closer look. Some models are slightly different but most include the following

- Your power port is usually either along the side or the rear
- Along the side you'll find your USB ports. How many you have will depend on the model but you'll usually find at least two.
- You'll also find an HDMI port either on the rear or along the side.
- 1/8th inch (3.5mm) headphone jack will usually be located along the side.
- Also you might find a card reader for SD cards usually used in most digital cameras.
- Along the top of your screen, you'll find a webcam and there will be a built in microphone there too, which comes in handy when you want to 'hang out' with your friends.

Chapter 1: What is a ChromeBook?

Your apps run in Google Chrome. You can write and edit documents using Google Docs, analyse numbers with Google Sheets SpreadSheet App, and create presentations using Google Slides. These work in a similar fashion to Microsoft Office.

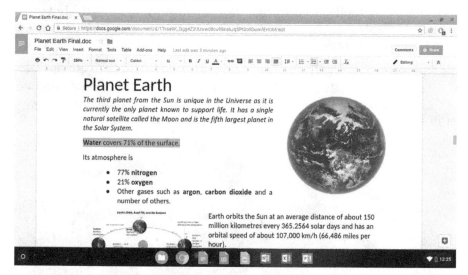

A Chromebook is known as a 'cloud device', meaning all your files, photographs and work are stored in the cloud and you work on your files online. All your files are stored on Google Drive.

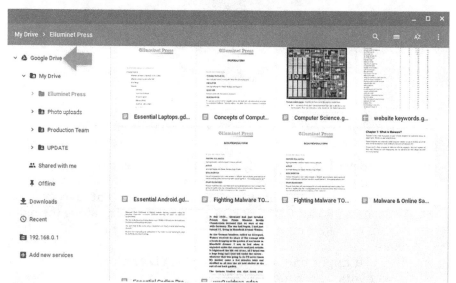

This is called cloud computing and allows on-demand access to a pool of computing resources such as apps, storage, email, social media and other services not stored locally on your device.

Chapter 1: What is a ChromeBook?

In the illustration, the lightning bolts represent a WiFi or 4G internet connection, and the cloud represents the cloud computing platform where all your email, photos, music, documents and social media are stored.

Virtually nothing is stored on your ChromeBook or phone, everything is stored in the cloud on large servers such as the ones below.

This means you can access your email, photos or do your work anywhere with an internet connection - you could be using your phone or ChromeBook to do this.

Setting up your ChromeBook

ChromeBooks are very easy to set up. They come pre-installed with Chrome OS that allows you to run your apps.

Creating a Google Account

If you use GMail or Google+ you will already have a Google Account. If this is the case, you don't need to create a new Google Account, so you can skip this step.

If you don't have one, you can create one online before you start, if you have another computer by opening your web browser and browsing to the following page

```
accounts.google.com/signup
```

Fill in your name in the first two frields, then under 'username', type in the name you want to appear in your email address. This can be a nickname, or your full name. The name must be unique, so if someone else has already taken the name, you'll need to choose a new one, or add a couple of numbers. Google will tell you if the username you entered has already been used.

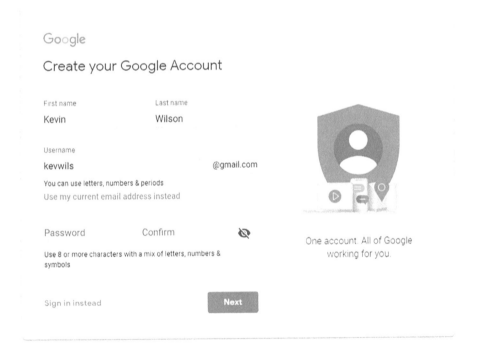

Enter the password you want to use in the 'password' field, then type it again to confirm it in the 'confirm' field.

Click 'next'.

Initial Setup

When you first turn on your ChromeBook, you'll come to the welcome screen. From here, select your language and your keyboard layout specific to your country.

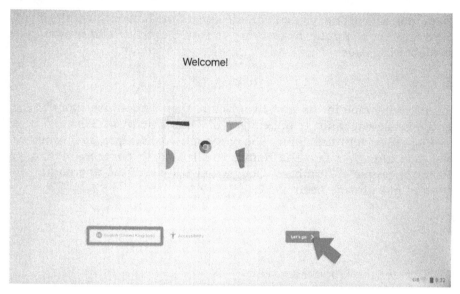

Once you have done that, select a network. This is usually your wifi network if you have one at home. This can also be a hotspot in a coffee shop, library, airport, office, school/college and so on.

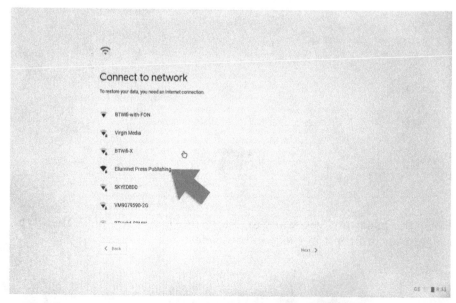

Enter your wifi password or key and click 'connect'. Your wifi network name and password/key is usually printed on the back of your router .

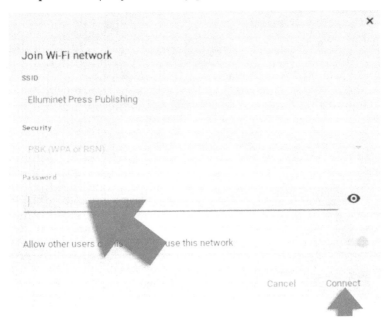

If you do not have access to wifi, you can buy a USB adapter or modem for your internet connection type. The one pictured below is for an ethernet cable and can be used with most cable modems.

Chapter 2: Setting up your ChromeBook

On the 'terms and conditions' page, turn off the 'optional. Help make Chrome OS better by automatically sending diagnostic and usage data to Google'. Then click 'accept and continue'.

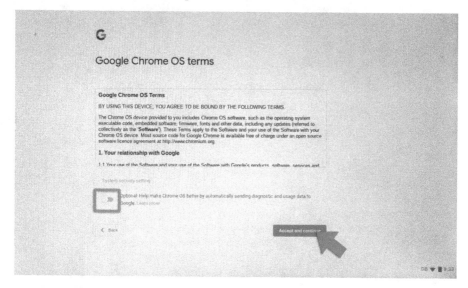

Next, enter your Google Account username and password. If you have a Gmail account or use Google+, then you will have a Google Account. Just enter these details and click 'next'.

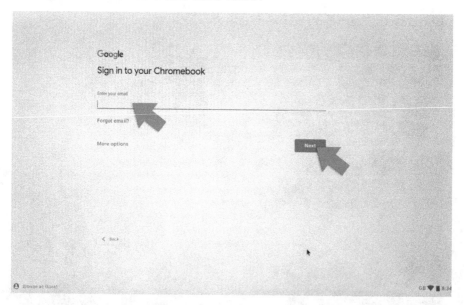

If you don't have one, click 'more options', then 'create new account' and enter your details as prompted.

On the last screen click 'accept and continue'.

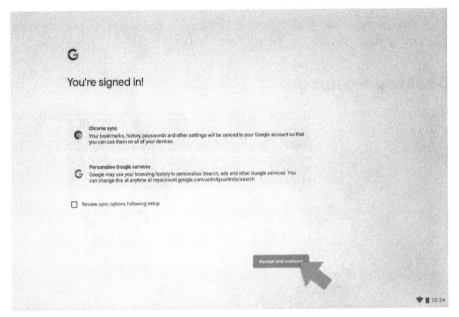

Once the setup is complete, you'll find yourself on the main desktop.

We'll take a look at getting around your ChromeBook desktop in chapter 3.

Personalise your ChromeBook

You can personalise your ChromeBook in a few ways; most obvious one being your desktop picture or wallpaper.

Desktop Wallpaper

Right click on your desktop. To do this, tap with two fingers on the touchpad.

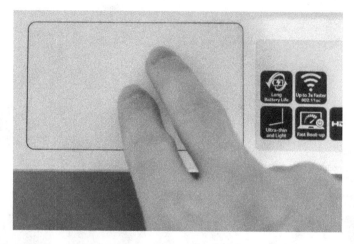

From the popup menu, select 'set wallpaper'.

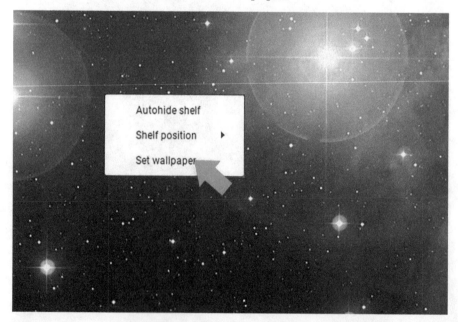

Autohide shelf

Shelf position ▶

Set wallpaper

You'll see some categories along the left hand side of the window, select one.

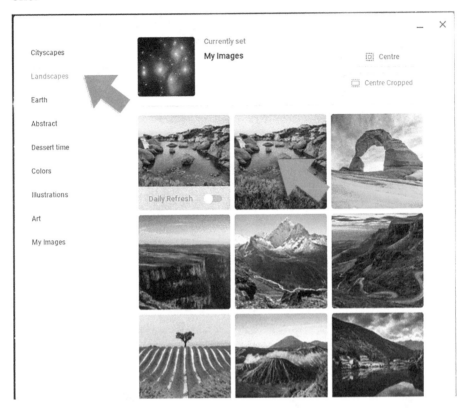

Scroll down the thumbnail previews of all the wallpapers and click on one you like.

Using your Own Photos

If you want to add your own image, open Google Drive in your file explorer.

You'll find your file explorer on the shelf along the bottom of the screen. If it isn't there, you'll find the icon on your launcher on the far left hand side.

Chapter 2: Setting up your ChromeBook

Browse through your photos - you'll find your photos in 'My Files' or 'Google Drive'.

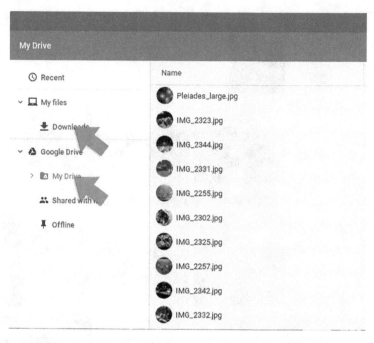

Right click on the one you want to use (to right click, tap on the image with two fingers on the touch pad).

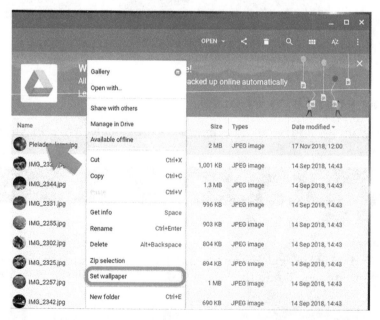

If the photo you want isn't there, it might be on Google Photos. To open Google Photos, click the launcher on the far left hand side of the screen.

Open the launcher to full screen

Click on Google Photos.

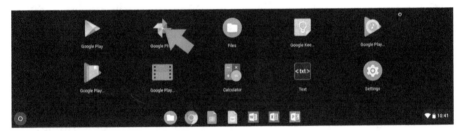

Browse through your photos. When you hover your mouse pointer over an image, you'll notice a small tick on the top left. Click on this to select the photo.

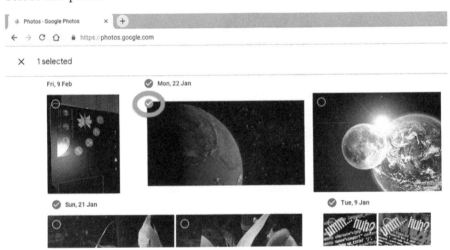

Chapter 2: Setting up your ChromeBook

Click the three dots icon on the top right, then from the drop down menu, select 'download'.

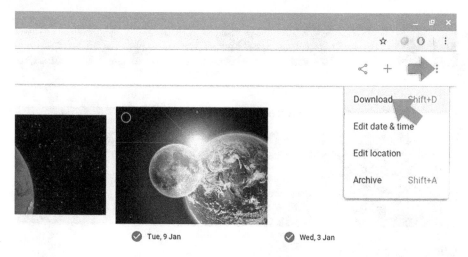

Open your file explorer from the shelf along the bottom of the screen.

Go to 'my files', then select 'downloads'. Right click on the photo you just downloaded, then from the popup menu, select 'set as wallpaper'.

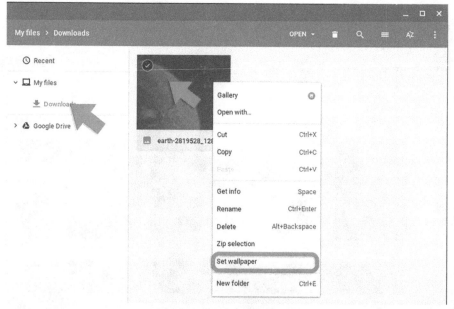

Transferring your Files to ChromeBook

There are various ways to transfer your files over to your ChromeBook.

Using Google Drive

You can upload files to Google Drive directly from your old computer or device.

Note with Google Drive you get 15GB free. If you need any more, you'll need to pay a subscription fee.

On your old computer, open your web browser and navigate to

`drive.google.com`

Sign in with your Google Account, then from the Google Drive home page, click 'my drive' on the left hand side of your browser window.

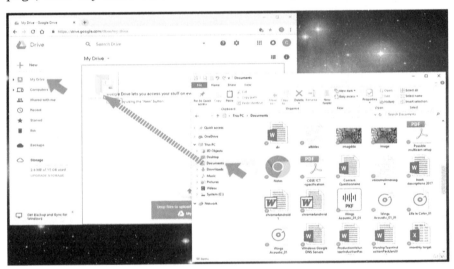

Now open file explorer and navigate to where your files are saved. This is usually under the 'this pc' section on the left hand side.

Click 'documents', then drag the folder over to the Google Drive home page, as shown above. It helps to position your windows side by side.

Do the same for any other folders such as 'pictures', 'music', and 'videos'. Allow the files to upload - it could take a while depending on the speed of your internet connection. Keep in mind that you can only upload 15GB of data. If you need more space you'll need to pay a subscription fee.

Using an External Drive

You can use a flash drive or external hard drive that has enough space to store your data.

Plug the external drive or flash drive into a USB port on your old computer. Then open up file explorer. Your external drive will show up as a USB Drive.

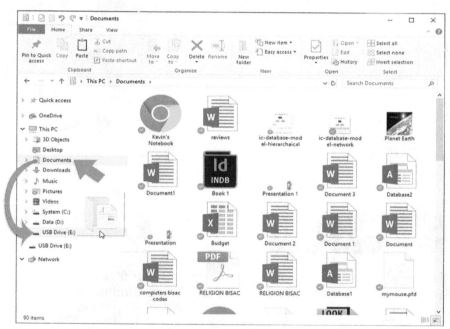

Navigate to where your files are saved. This is usually under the 'this pc' section on the left hand side.

Click 'documents', then drag the folder over to the USB Drive, as shown above. Do the same for any other folders such as 'pictures', 'music', and 'videos'.

Once the files have finished copying, remove the drive from your old computer and plug it into a USB port on your ChromeBook.

Now, on your ChromeBook, open 'files' from the app shelf. You'll also find it on your launcher.

Select your USB drive from the panel on the left hand side of the window.

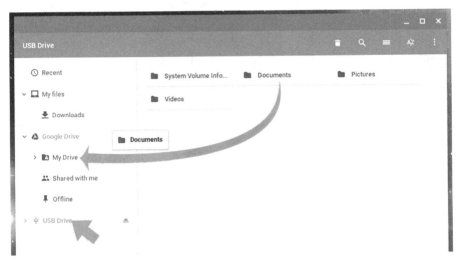

Click and drag the 'documents' folder to 'google drive'. Do the same with the rest of the folders you copied from your old device.

Setting up Printers

If you have a fairly modern printer - such as a wireless printer, you can usually add it with no problem. Traditional and older printers can still be used but are a bit more temperamental to add.

Cloud Enabled Wireless Printers

Your printer needs to support Google Cloud Print - you can check this in the documentation that came with your printer.

Turn on your printer and make sure it's connected to your WiFi.

On your ChromeBook, click the clock on the bottom right to open the system tray, then click the 'settings' icon.

Scroll down to the bottom of the page and click 'advanced'.

Scroll down to the 'printing' settings, then click 'Google Cloud Print'.

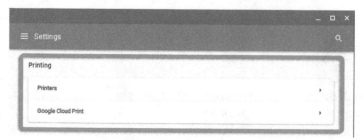

Under the 'google cloud print' settings, click 'manage cloud print devices'.

Your ChromeBook will scan for new devices. Any cloud enabled printers it finds will be listed under 'new devices'.

Click 'register' next to the printer's name.

It will take a few moments for your printer to be added. Once the setup is complete, you'll see your printer listed under 'my devices'.

Devices

New devices

Classic printers
You can add classic printers connected to your computer to Google Cloud Print.

Add printers

My devices

HP ENVY 5020 [30055c803]   Manage
HP [30055c803]

Save to Google Drive   Manage
Save your document as a PDF in Google Drive

Traditional Printers

If your printer is a bit older and isn't cloud enabled, you can plug it into your ChromeBook using a USB cable. This is the simplest way to connect an older printer.

First, plug your printer into your ChromeBook using a USB cable.

On your ChromeBook, click the clock on the bottom right of your screen to open the system tray.

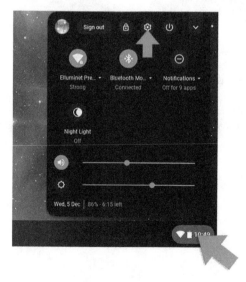

Then click the settings icon. Scroll down and click 'advanced'.

Scroll down to the 'printing' settings, then click 'printers'.

Click 'add printer'.

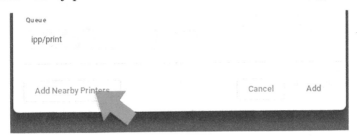

Click 'add nearby printers' on the bottom left of the dialog box.

Your ChromeBook will scan for 'near by' printers, or printers that are plugged into your ChromeBook. This process can be a bit temperamental, especially with older printers, so you may need to refresh the settings screen using the refresh button on the top row of the keyboard.

Once detected, your printer will be listed. Click on it, then select 'add' on the bottom right.

Adding Bluetooth Devices

You can add bluetooth mice, headphones, keyboards to your ChromeBook. This process is called pairing.

To add a bluetooth device, you need to put the device into pairing mode. To do this, press the pairing button on the bottom of the device - you might need to read the device's instructions on how to do this.

In this example, I'm going to add a bluetooth mouse. First power the mouse on and press the pairing button underneath. The light will begin to flash.

On your ChromeBook, click on the clock on the bottom right to open the system tray.

Select the bluetooth icon and turn it on if it isn't already.

Allow your ChromeBook to scan for nearby devices, this will take a minute or two. Once a device has been found, it will appear in the list.

Click on the device in the list to connect it.

Pair Bluetooth device   ✕

Connecting to 'Bluetooth Mouse'

Cancel

Once your ChromeBook has made a connection, you can use your device as normal.

Chapter 3

Getting around ChromeBook

ChromeBooks are very easy to navigate and are build around the Chrome Web Browser. So if you're familiar with browsing the web, you'll be able to use your ChromeBook with little difficulty.

First thing you'll need to do, if you haven't already done so, is sign in with your Google Account email and password.

Power Up & Power Down

To power up your ChromeBook, press the power key on the top right hand side of the keyboard. The Chrome logo will appear on the screen while the system starts.

To shut down your ChromeBook, hold the power button for 1 second, you'll see three options pop up onto the screen.

Click 'power off' to shut down your ChromeBook. Click 'sign out' to sign out of your account and return to the login screen. Click 'lock screen' to lock your screen - useful if you are working on something and need to quickly lock your screen if you need to leave your ChromeBook for a few minutes without having to sign out completely.

If your ChromeBook has frozen or crashed, hold the power key until the screen goes blank. Wait a few seconds, then press the power key again to start up your ChromeBook

35

The Login Screen

The login screen, sometimes called the lock screen, is the first screen you'll see when you turn on your ChromeBook. Along the bar at the bottom, you'll see a few icons. From here, you can shut your ChromeBook down, allow someone to browse as a guest (without a Google Account) and add a new user with a Google Account to your ChromeBook.

On the bottom right of the screen, you'll see your wifi settings, battery and the clock. Click on this to reveal the options menu, where you can change wifi network, accessibility, volume and brightness controls.

In the centre of the screen, you'll see your user account you registered when you set up your ChromeBook. Enter your password to log in.

Once your ChromeBook is set up, you will need to log in with your Google Account, so on the login screen, enter your password.

Before we go any further, lets take a look at some navigation features we can use to get around the user interface of your ChromeBook.

The Touch Pad

If you have used a laptop before, then you'll be familiar with the touch pad or track pad.

You can use your fingers to move your pointer around the screen using what are called gestures.

One Finger Tap

This is like your left mouse button and can be used to select objects such as icons or text fields on the screen. Just tap your finger on the pad.

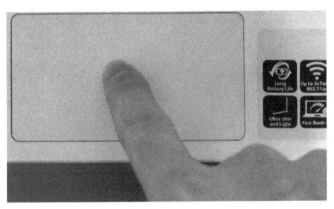

Two Finger Tap

This is like the right mouse button and can be used to right click on objects such as icons to reveal a context menu of options. Just tap both fingers on the pad at the same time.

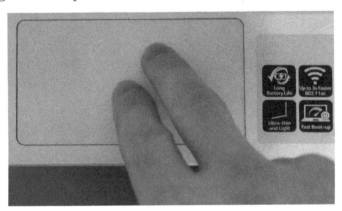

One Finger Click and Drag

Position your pointer on to an object such as window title bar, or image on your screen, then press your finger on the touch pad until you hear a click, then without releasing your finger, drag across the track pad to move the object.

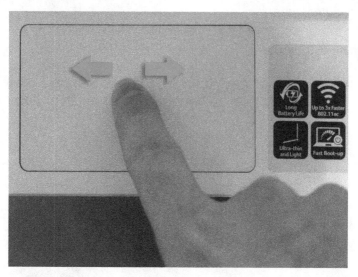

Two Finger Scroll

You can use two fingers on the track pad to scroll up and down windows, web pages, maps and so on.

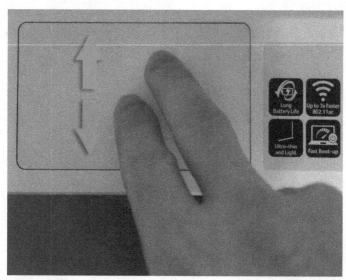

Two Finger Swipe

While you are browsing the web, you can go back to a previous page by swiping your two fingers to the left on the track pad and advance forward a page you have visited by swiping to the right.

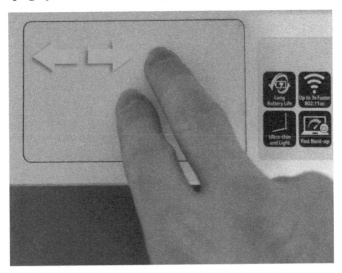

Three Finger Swipe

You can quickly display all your open apps by swiping your three fingers downwards on the track pad.

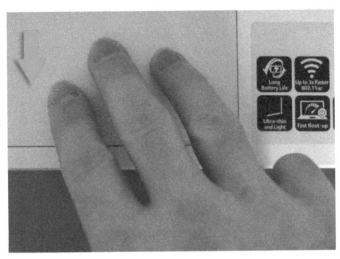

You'll see any open apps show up as thumbnail previews. You can click on these to open them or close them down.

The Keyboard

Here is a typical ChromeBook keyboard. It looks like a conventional keyboard you'll find on any computer, but it's worth noting the keys along the top.

Along the top of your keyboard, you'll see some special keys. These help when using the Chrome web browser.

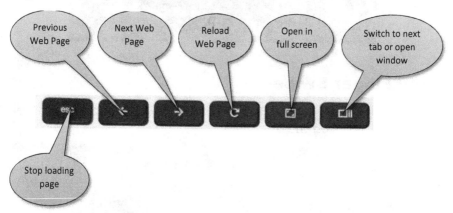

Towards the right hand side of the row, you'll see some keys that allow you to change the brightness of the screen and adjust audio volume.

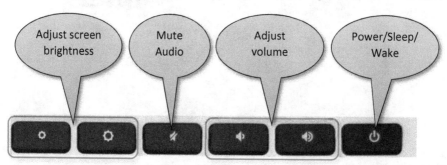

Onscreen Keyboard Help

Press **ctrl alt ?** to reveal the help screen.

Now hold down the ctrl key and you'll see all the keyboard shortcuts highlighted on the keyboard.

You can also press alt or shift to see those keyboard shortcuts.

ChromeBook Task Manager

Hold down the **search** key, then tap **escape**. The search key looks like a small magnifying glass, you'll find it on the left hand side of your keyboard. On the old ChromeBooks press shift-escape.

You'll see a window pop up with a list of tasks (apps) that are currently running, as well as how much memory and cpu time they're using.

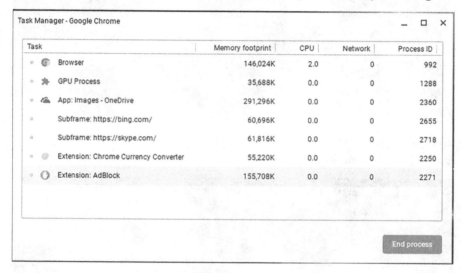

The task manager is useful if an app is not responding or has crashed.

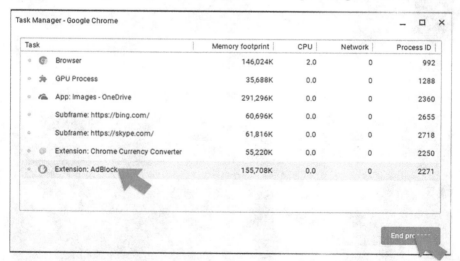

Just click on the task (app) in the list, then click 'end process'. The non-responsive app is usually labelled 'not responding'.

Adding Users

As mentioned earlier, you can add two types of users to your ChromeBook.

The first is a guest. This allows any user to get onto your ChromeBook without having to sign in with a Google Account. Guest users do *not* have access to the app store, Google+ or a Google email account, they can pretty much just browse the internet.

The other type, is a user with a Google Account. This is useful if more than one person uses your ChromeBook and need access to their own email, apps, and files. This is the recommended way to use your ChromeBook.

Add User with a Google Account

Users with a Google Account can access the full range of apps, use their email, Google+ and purchase apps from the App Store. Click 'add person' from the login screen.

Allow them to sign in with their Google Account username and password.

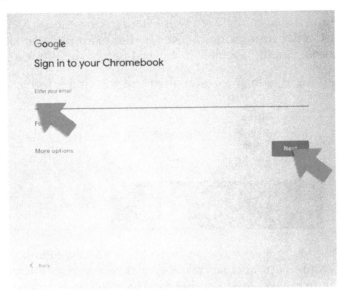

Click 'next'.

Desktop and the App Shelf

The desktop looks similar to a lot of operating systems out there, you have a background image or wallpaper and along the bottom you have what Google calls the App Shelf. This is very much like the task bar found in Windows 10 or the App Dock found on a Mac.

On the left hand side of the app shelf you have what looks like a magnifying glass icon. This is your App Launcher and allows you to open any app that has been added to your ChromeBook, as well as searching the web.

The next icon along is the Google Chrome web browser. This works just like any web browser you would find on a PC or Mac and allows you to search the web, use web apps, and use the internet how you would on any other computer.

The space on the app shelf after the Google Chrome icon can be for pinning any other app for quick access. For example, you could add, Google Photos, Gmail, Google Drive, word processing apps and so on.

On the right hand side of the app shelf you will find a few small icons.

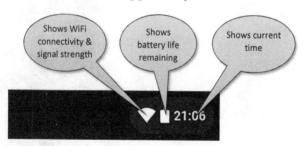

The first one along shows notifications such as new emails or system messages, reminders and so on. The next one across shows WiFi or ethernet connectivity. Next you have an icon for battery level, and the clock. Click on the icon to reveal the system tray.

System Tray & Notifications

The system tray contains all your controls to connect to a WiFi network, pair a bluetooth device such as a mouse, change audio volume, screen brightness, sign in & out, shut down ChromeBook, as well as access the system settings, and display notification messages.

To reveal the system tray, click on the clock status icon on the bottom right of your screen.

Along the top of the system tray, you'll see all the system notifications. Click on them to view details, or click 'clear all' to clear them.

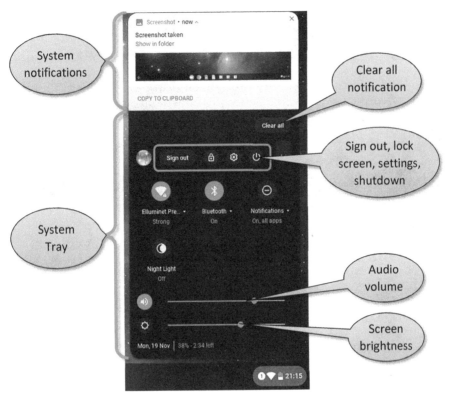

Underneath you'll see your system controls. Here you can sign out, lock your screen or shut down your ChromeBook, as well as connect to WiFi networks, bluetooth devices, control the brightness and volume and access system settings.

App Launcher

The App Launcher is very much like your start menu in Windows and is where you will find all the apps that have been installed on your ChromeBook.

To reveal the App Launcher, click the circle icon on the bottom left of your screen.

Click the arrow on the top middle of the launcher to open it up.

From here, you can search the web by entering a web site address or some keywords as you would normally do when using Google Search.

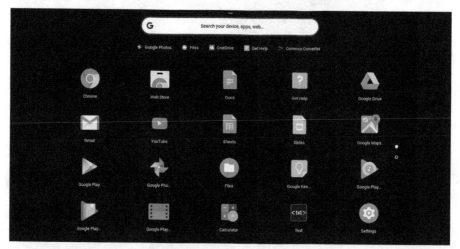

Below this, you'll see icons representing the apps installed on your ChromeBook.

Scroll up and down to see apps on the additional pages if required.

Click on an icon to start the app.

Pin Apps to your App Shelf

The app shelf is similar to the task bar in Windows 10 and you can pin app icons to this shelf for quick access. So you can add all your most used apps to this shelf and click them when you need them.

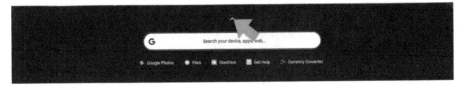

To do this, open up your App Launcher and click the arrow at the top to reveal all the apps.

From this window, right click on the app icon you want to pin to your shelf.

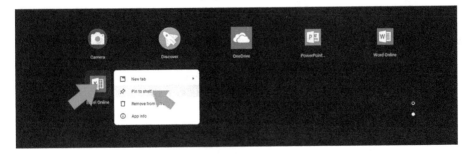

From the popup menu, click on 'pin to shelf'. You will see the app icon appear on the shelf at the bottom left of the screen, as shown below.

You can do this for all your most used apps, allowing you to quickly launch an app directly from the app shelf.

Chapter 4

Using Apps

There are two types of app for the ChromeBook: a hosted app and a packaged app. A hosted app or Chrome app as it is sometimes called, is an app that will run within the Chrome Web Browser. A packaged app is very similar to the traditional desktop apps we see in Windows and Mac operating systems, and is capable of interacting directly with hardware and storage on your ChromeBook. These apps are available from the Chrome Web Store.

Also more recently Google have added the ability to run Android Apps from the Google Play Store. The latest ChromeBooks will be able to run most of these apps. Older ChromeBooks may not run Android apps at all.

Chrome Web Store

This is where you can download countless apps for your ChromeBook. Many of these apps are free, but there are one or two that you will have to pay for.

To launch the website, open your app launcher

Click the arrow at the top to open the launcher fully. Click 'web store'.

Once the web store opens, you'll see the home screen. Here, you can browse for apps and search for specific apps.

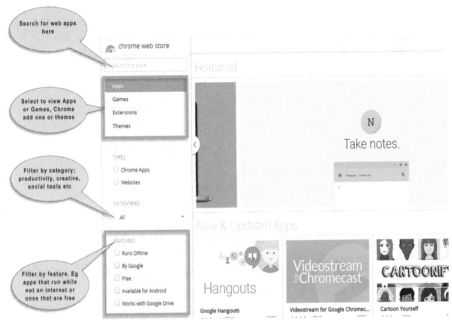

Chapter 4: Using Apps

Browsing the Store

Down the left hand side of the Web Store, you'll see some options. Here you can select 'extensions', which are small apps that run within the Chrome Web Browser and extend the browser's features.

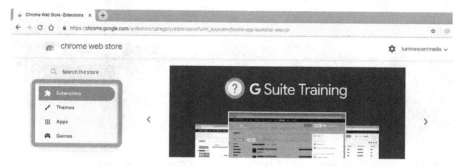

You can also select 'themes', which change the way your ChromeBook looks by changing the desktop wallpaper, toolbar colours, on screen fonts and so on.

You can select 'apps', such as Google Docs that either run on your ChromeBook itself or within the Chrome Web Browser.

You can also select 'games', which are gaming apps that run on your ChromeBook or Chrome Web Browser.

For the sake of this example, I'm going to select 'apps' from the options.

Underneath that, you can select various categories. To open the list of categories, click on the drop down box under 'categories' on the left hand side of your screen. Click on one of the categories. So if you are looking for productivity apps such as word processors, lifestyle apps such as social media, or educational apps, you'll find them here.

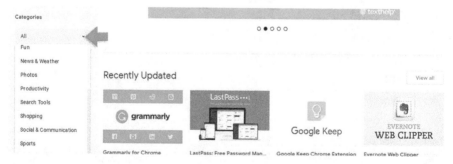

For this example, I'm going to select 'productivity' from the list of categories.

Many of the categories are divided into sub categories. So in our example, the productivity category is sub divided into 'creative tools' such as graphics and drawing, 'developer tools' such as coding and app development, 'office applications' such as word processors and spreadsheets, 'search & browsing tools' such as web browsers, and 'task management' such as todo lists.

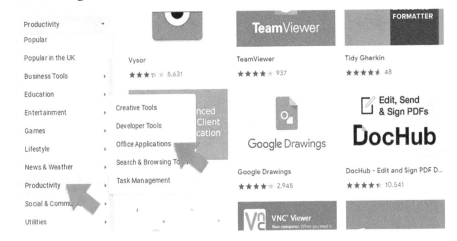

I'm going to select 'office applications'. Here, you'll see all your office applications such as word processors and any tools you need to get your work done on your ChromeBook.

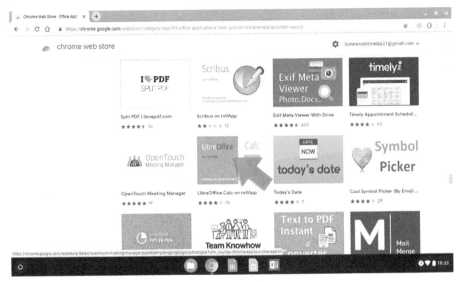

Scroll down and have a look at the apps. Just click on one of the thumbnails to see details on the app, and add it to your ChromeBook.

Chapter 4: Using Apps

Searching the Store

On the top left hand side of the store, you'll see a search field.

Click in the search field and type what you're looking for. You can use the app's name if you know it, or you can type something more generic such as 'word processing', or 'social media'. You'll also see a list of suggestions appear as you type - you can click any of these. Press the enter key on your keyboard to execute the search.

The Web Store will return a list of apps matching your search. You'll see the most popular apps in the list. To see all the apps, click 'more extensions' or 'more apps' on the top right of the screen.

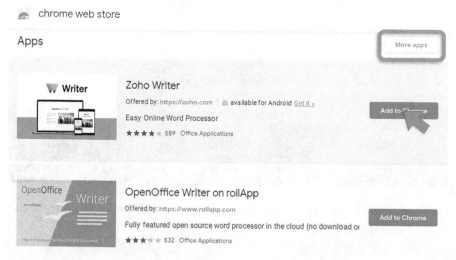

Downloading New Apps

Downloading new apps is fairly straightforward. Once you have searched for and found the app you want, click on the thumbnail icon.

Once the info screen appears, you'll see a write up of the app with some screen shots and features. On the top right of your screen, you'll see a couple of icons. To install the app tap 'add to chrome'

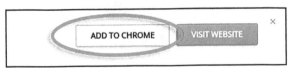

Then click 'add app' to install

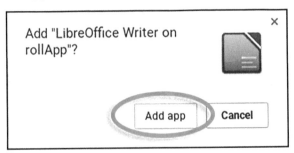

You will see the app icon added to your App Launcher.

Managing Apps

Over time, Apps and Chrome Extensions can start to fill up your ChromeBook, making it sluggish and unresponsive. It's a good idea to remove apps and extensions you don't use.

Removing Apps

To remove an app, open your app launcher from the bottom left hand side of the screen. Click the arrow in the centre to reveal all your apps.

Right click on the app you want to remove.

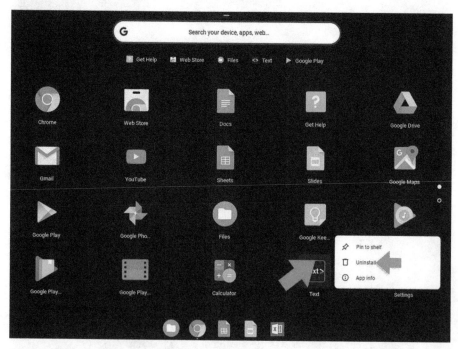

From the popup menu, click 'uninstall'.

Do this for all the apps you want to remove.

Removing Chrome Extensions

To remove a Chrome Extension, open the Chrome Browser from the app launcher.

Click the three dots icon on the top right. From the drop down menu, click 'more tools', then select 'extensions'.

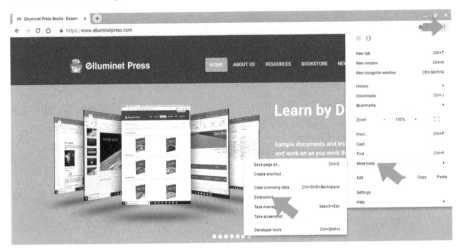

You'll see a list of all the extensions that have been added to Chrome.

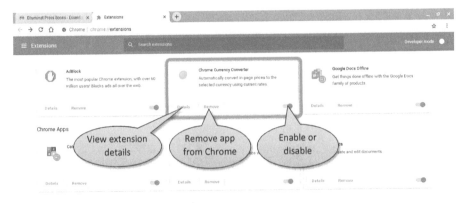

Click 'remove' under the extension you want to remove.

Web, Email & Communication

The heart of the ChromeBook is the Chrome Web Browser, this is what you'll use to browse the web and use certain extensions and apps.

GMail will allow you to check your Google Email, as well as send & receive email messages

Hangouts is for video chat and conferencing.

Google Chrome

You'll find Google Chrome on your app shelf along the bottom of your screen.

You'll also find it on your app launcher.

Once Chrome starts up, you'll see the main screen similar to the one below.

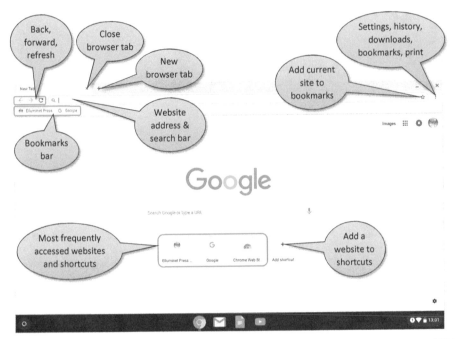

Chapter 5: Web, Email & Communication

Browser Tabs

Browser tabs help you to keep track of websites you have open instead of having multiple browser windows open at the same time. This makes it easier to see what sites are open and switch between them.

You'll find your browser tabs along the top of the screen. In this example there are three different websites open in three different tabs.

When you want to open a new website, click on the new tab icon.

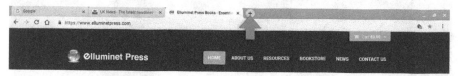

Enter the website address or Google search. You can also select one of your shortcuts under the Google search bar, or select a bookmark from the bookmarks bar along the top.

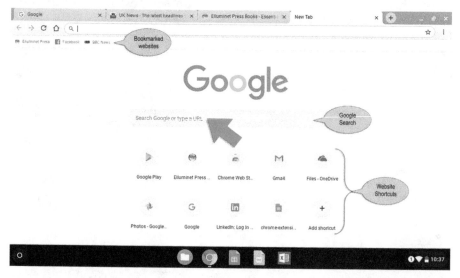

To return to any of the other websites, just click on the tab at the top of the screen.

To close a tab, just click the small x on the right hand side of the tab you want to close.

Browse Incognito

This mode is useful if you don't want Google Chrome on your ChromeBook to record your browsing activity, such as website history, cookies, site data, or information entered into forms. This mode doesn't hide your activity from your ISP, school/college, or employer.

To open an incognito tab, click the three dots icon on the top right of your screen

A new window will popup telling you you've gone icognito.

Type the web address of the site you want to visit, or a Google search into the field at the top of the screen.

Browsing History

The browsing history keeps a list of all the websites you've visited with Google Chrome. To find your browser history, click the three dots icon on the top right of your screen and select 'history' from the drop down menu.

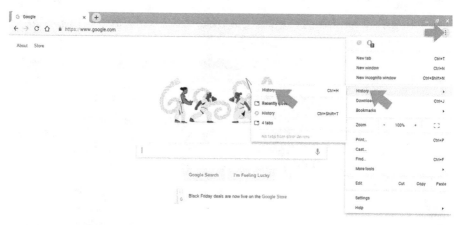

A new tab will pop up. From here, you can scroll down and click any site to revisit.

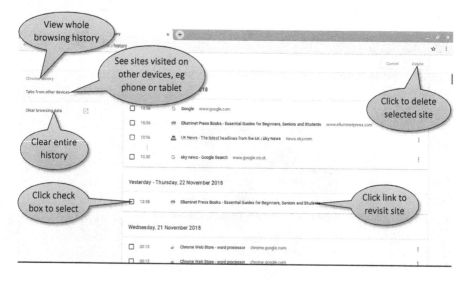

To delete a site from the history, click the tick box next to the website in the list, then click 'delete' on the top right.

Click 'clear history' to clear the list of visited websites, cache, cookies, and other site data.

Bookmarking a Site

It is useful to bookmark, or favourite a site you visit frequently. To do this, navigate to the website you want to bookmark, then click the small star icon to the right of the address bar at the top of your window.

Enter a meaningful name in the 'name' field, if there isn't one. Add your bookmark to the bookmarks bar along the top of your screen.

Click 'done' when you're finished.

Notice that your bookmarks bar isn't enabled by default. To enable the bar, click the three dots icon on the top right of the screen. From the drop down, go to 'bookmarks', then from the slideout menu, select 'show bookmarks bar'.

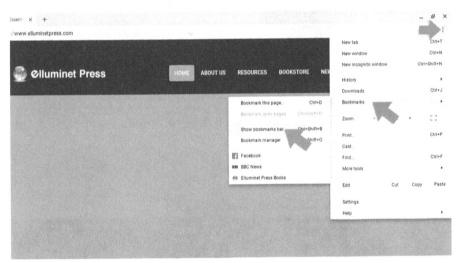

The bar will appear along the top of the screen underneath the address bar.

Bookmark Folders

If you have a lot of bookmarked sites, the bookmarks bar can become very cluttered. To get around this, you can create folders on your bookmarks bar, to make it easier to find sites.

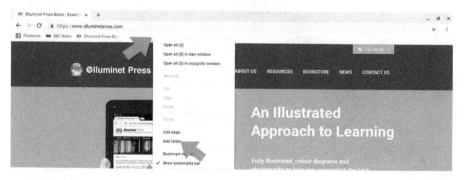

In the dialog box, type in the name of the folder and select 'bookmarks bar'.

Click 'save' when you're done. You'll see your folder appear on the bookmarks bar.

Now you can drag the site bookmarks you want to put in this folder. For example, I'm going to add 'facebook' to the social media folder.

Site Shortcuts

Site shortcuts appear on your home page - the page that appears when you open Chrome or when you open a new tab.

To add a shortcut, you need to know the websites address or URL. For example, I want to add the Elluminet Press website to the shortcuts. To do this, click 'add shortcut' from Chrome's home screen. In the dialog box that appears, type in the website's name and address.

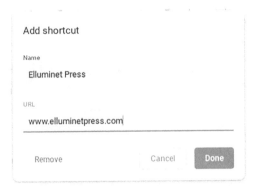

To delete a shortcut, hover your mouse pointer over the shortcut's icon on the Chrome home screen. You'll see three dots appear on the top right. Click on this icon.

From the popup, click 'remove'.

63

Downloads

If you have downloaded photos, files, or web pages for offline viewing, you'll find them here in the downloads folder. To get to your downloads, click the '3 dots' icon on the top right. From the menu that appears, select 'downloads'.

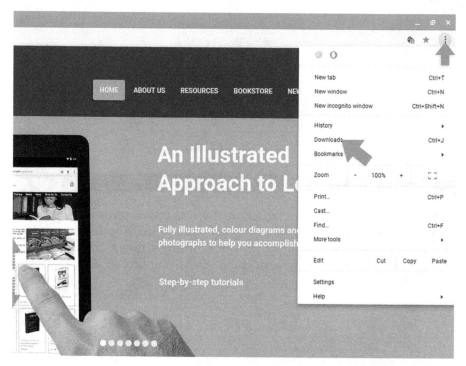

Here you'll see a reverse chronological list of items you've downloaded.

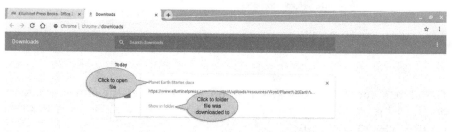

Click on an item in the list to open it up.

Printing a Webpage

To print a webpage in Chrome, click the three dots icon on the top right of your screen, then from the drop down menu, select 'print'.

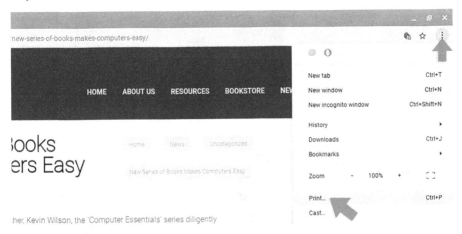

Check the printer 'destination', make sure your printer is selected. Click 'change' if you need to change this. Enter the pages you want to print, or leave it blank to print all of them. Enter the number of copies you want.

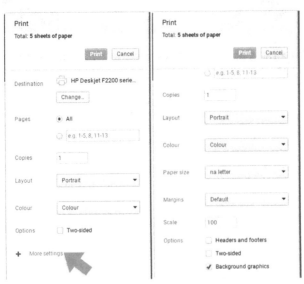

Click 'more settings'. Select the paper size if needed. Change the margins if the website doesn't fit on the page. Click 'background graphics' - this ensures all the graphics will print.

Click 'print' when you're done.

Google Mail

Also known as GMail and is where you'll be able to check your email. You'll find Google Main on your app launcher.

Open the app launcher fully and click the GMail icon.

Once GMail opens, you'll be able to see the email messages sent to your Google Account email address. Let's take a look at the main screen.

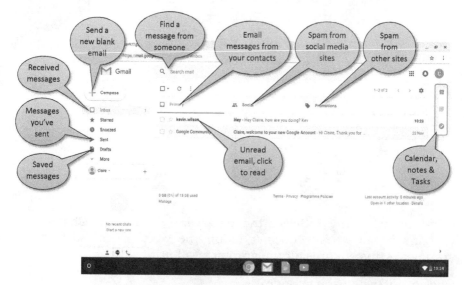

Reading Mail

When you open GMail it will check for email, any new messages will appear in your inbox. Click on the message in your inbox. The contents will be displayed in the main window.

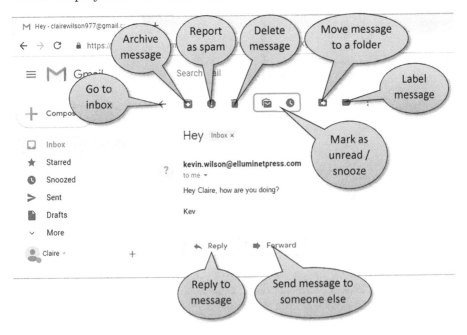

Writing a New Message

To start a new message, click 'compose' on the top left hand side of the main screen.

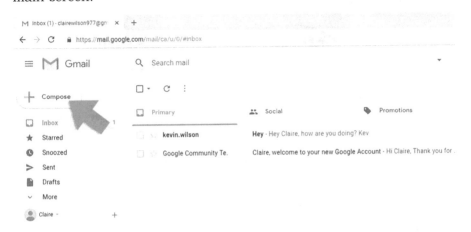

In the message popup window, you will need to enter the person's email address in the 'To' field.

Add a subject, then type your message in the body section.

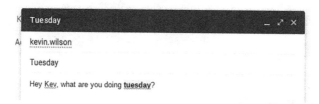

In the body section, you can use the normal text formatting tools such as bold, change the font colour or size and so on, using the format tool bar as you can see below.

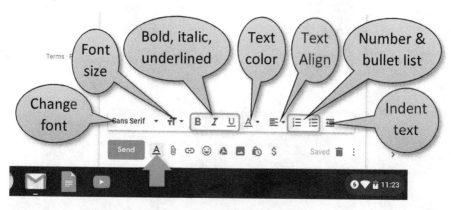

Hit 'send' on bottom left to send your message.

Reply to a Message

To reply to the message, click the reply icon on the bottom of the email.

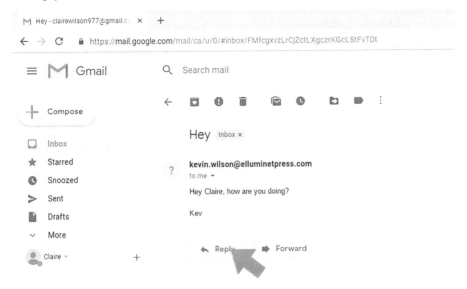

You'll see a screen that looks a bit like a word processor. Here you can type in your message. Your message will appear under the message you're replying to, as shown below.

You can use the basic formatting tools. You can make text bold - select the text and click the 'A' icon on the toolbar.

Click 'send' when you're done.

Adding Attachments

To attach a file, click the paperclip icon along the bottom of your message. Use this option to attach files such as documents, videos, music, or multiple photos.

Select your file from the dialog box. Click the tick box on the top left of the images to select multiple files. Click 'open' when you're done.

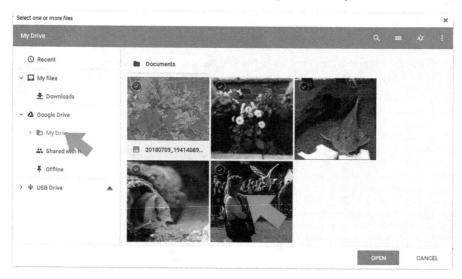

These attachments will be added to the end of the email.

Once you are done, click 'send' on the bottom left.

Inserting Images

Inserting images is a little different from adding an attachment. When you insert an image, you insert it into the body of the email message so it appears inline with the text.

In your email message, click the images icon from the bottom of your message.

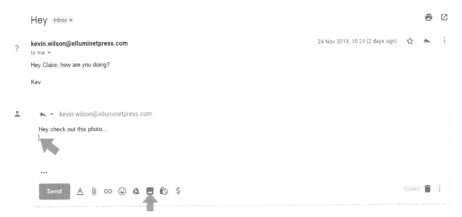

Click 'upload' along the top of the window, if it isn't already selected. Select 'inline' from the two options on the bottom right of the window.

Click 'choose photos to upload'.

Select your file from the dialog box. Click the tick box on the top left of the images to select multiple files. Click 'open' when you're done.

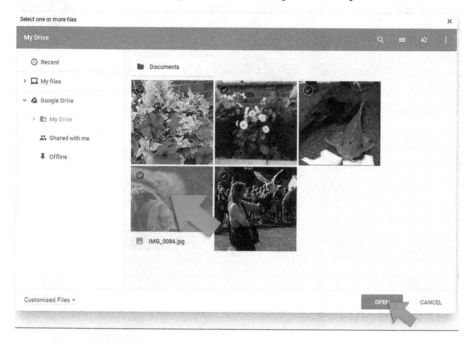

Notice the photo has been inserted within the text body of your email, rather than just attached to the end as an attachment.

Click the 'send' icon on the top right when you're done.

Sending Money

You can send money to someone using Google Pay. To use this feature, you'll need to have a payment method set up on your Google Account.

To send money, click the $ or £ icon on the bottom of your message.

Enter the amount you want to send and choose a payment method or add a new one.

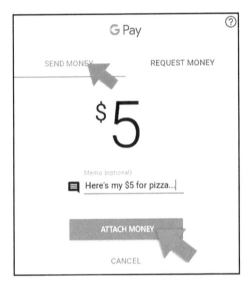

Click 'attach money'. If you don't have a payment method set up on your Google Account, click 'add debit card' then enter your card details.

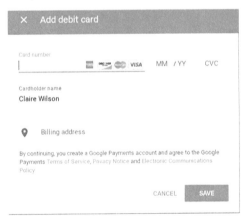

You'll see the Google Pay attachment at the bottom of your email. Click 'send' on the bottom left to send the message.

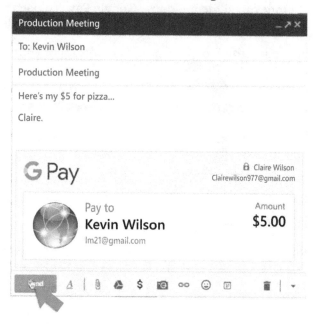

Now, when the recipient checks their email, they'll get a message like this in their inbox.

To claim the money, click 'claim money' at the bottom of the message.

Once you've claimed your money, it will be available in your Google Pay Balance. Go to

pay.Google.com

From here you'll be able to send money to other people, transfer to your bank account, or use it on the Google Play Store.

Adding Other Email Accounts

In the top right, click the 'settings' icon, then select 'settings' from the menu.

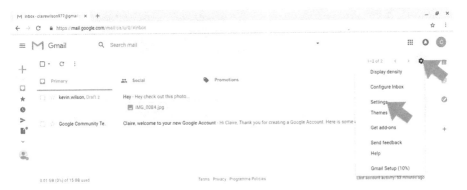

Click 'accounts and import', then select 'add an email account'.

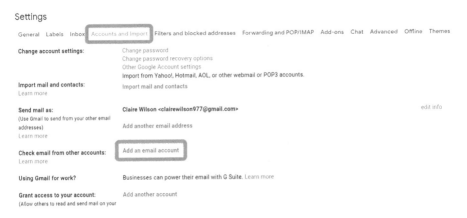

In the dialog box that appears, enter the email address of the account you want to add.

Click 'next'.

Select 'link accounts with Gmailify' if available, then click 'next'.

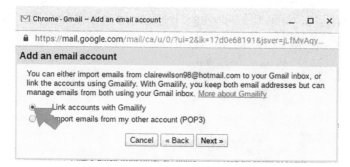

Sign in with the password for the account you're adding.

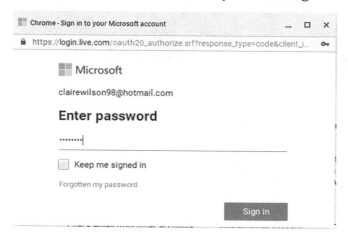

Click 'yes' to grant access to the email account you're adding.

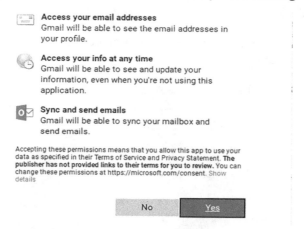

Click 'close' on the last dialog box, and you're done.

Contacts

The contacts app is your address book and contains your contact's email addresses, phone numbers and addresses.

You'll find Google Contacts in GMail. First open the GMail App from your app launcher.

Click the apps icon on the top right of your screen

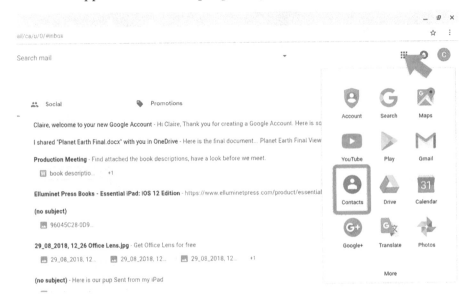

Click on the contacts icon.

View Contact Details

Once the contacts app opens, you'll see a list of all the people you have contact information for. Click on one of the names to view or edit the details for that person. I'm going to click on my contact 'Sophie' in the list.

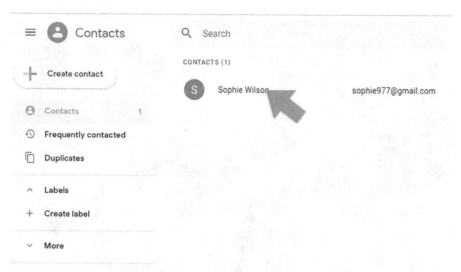

The person's details will open up on your screen.

Along the top you'll see three small icons on the right hand side. Here you can add the person to your favourites - the star icon. This is similar to your 'speed dial' on your phone, where you can quickly send messages to people you correspond with the most.

Click the pencil icon to edit the person's details, eg if they've changed their number or email address.

Use the three dots icon to open the drop down options menu. Here you can delete the contact, export, hide, or print the details.

Edit Details

Click on the name of the person in the list whose details you want to change.

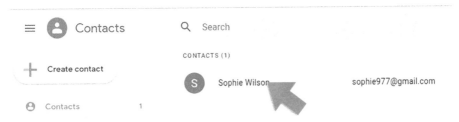

Click the pencil icon on the top right of the dialog box.

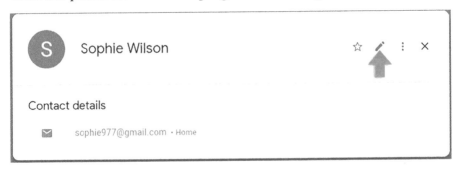

Click on the field you want to change. In this example I'm adding a mobile phone number.

Make any other changes you need to, then click 'save'.

79

Add New Contact

You can add a new contact from scratch using the contacts app. To do this, click 'create contact' on the top left of your screen.

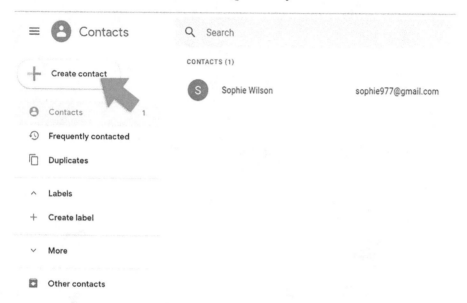

Enter the details into the appropriate fields, as shown below.

Click on the image on the top left to add a profile picture.

Click 'save' when you're done.

Add Contact from Message

You can add a new contact from the Hangouts App or the GMail App

Open the email.

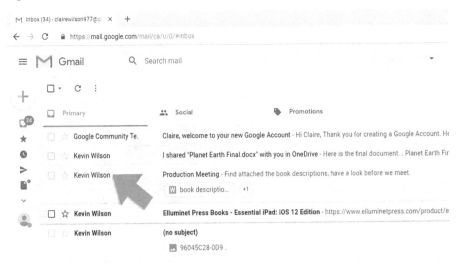

Click on the three dots icon on the top right of your email message, then select 'add ... to contacts list'.

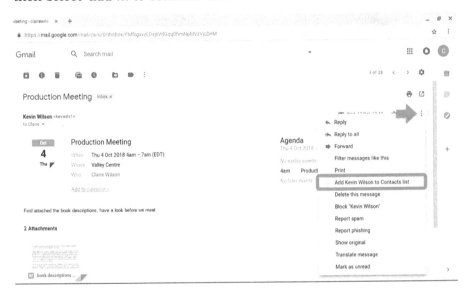

The email address and the person's name will be added to your contacts. Click on the contact's name in your contacts app to edit any details.

Calendar

The calendar app allows you to keep track of events and appointments. You can add reminders, create appointments and events, so you never miss anything.

To start the calendar app, open your GMail app from the app launcher.

Click the apps icon on the top right of your screen, then select 'calendar'.

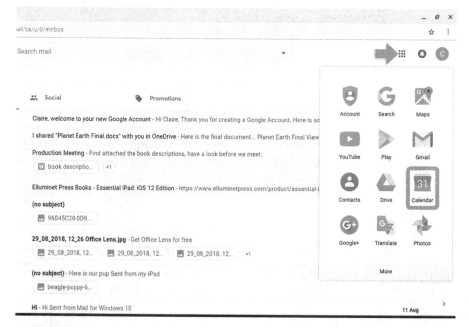

Calendar View

You can change the calendar view to show appointments and events by month, week or day - as shown below.

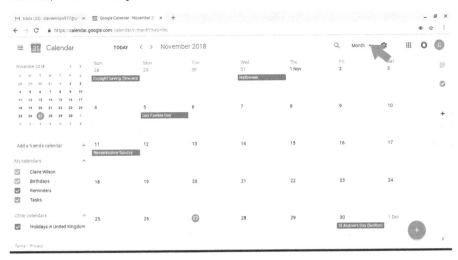

To do this, click the icon on the top right of the screen.

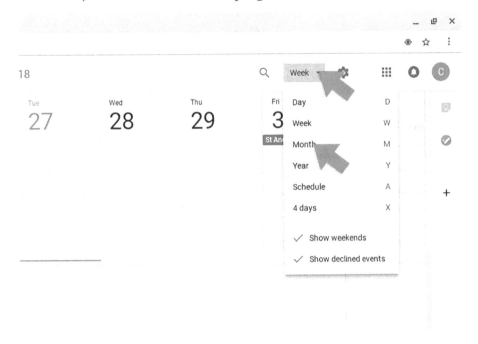

From the drop down menu, select 'day', 'week' or 'month', depending on how you want to view your events/appointments.

Add Event

To add a new event, reminder or appointment, in month view, click on the day the appointment falls on.

In the popup box, start typing in the name of the event or appointment in the field at the top. Eg "production meeting", "coffee with claire", and so on. Select 'event', then click 'more options'.

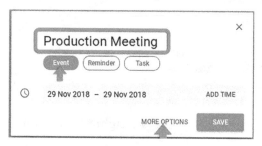

Remove the tick from 'all day' and enter the start and finish times of the event.

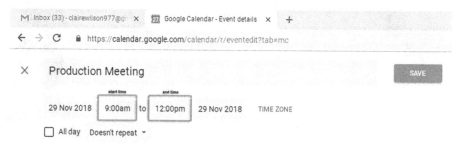

If this event repeats, for example, a weekly meeting, click where it says 'doesn't repeat' and from the drop down, select how often the event repeats. This event occurs every week, so I'm going to select 'weekly'.

Now select where the event/appointment will be held. Type in the location.

Google will search for places you've been, go to frequently, or places nearby. Click on one of these. So if we were meeting at the Valley Centre, I'd click on 'valley centre' in the list.

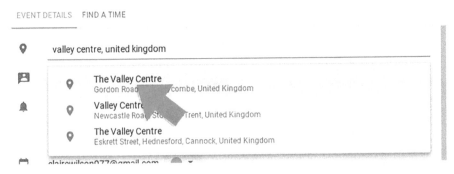

You'll see a summary of the appointment. Here you can amend any details, set a reminder - where it says 'notification', change the times - select how far in advance you want to be reminded. In this example, I've set it to remind me a day before. You can also set it to 30 mins before, an hour before, and so on.

Now we need to say who we are meeting. Click where it says 'add guests' on the right hand side.

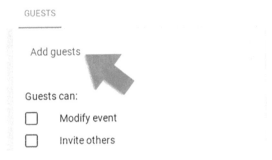

Start typing in the names of the people you want to send an invite to. You'll see a list of your contacts - select their name.

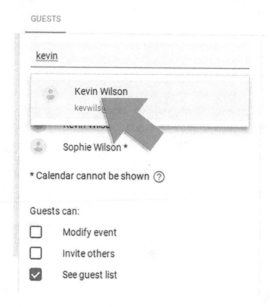

Underneath where it says 'guests can', remove the ticks from the permissions to prevent your guests from making changes to the event invitation. You can allow them to 'see the guest list' so they can see who is attending.

At the bottom left, where it says 'add description'. Add a message, and any attachments, or documents needed for the event. These could be minutes, meeting notes, programmes, and so on. To add an attachment, click the paper-clip icon, then select a file to attach.

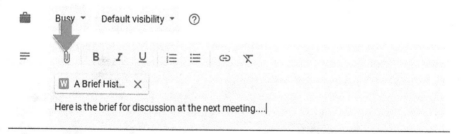

Click the blue 'save' button on the top right when you're done.

Click 'send' to send the invitations to your attendees if you added any guests.

Click 'invite' to allow your attendees to access any files you attached.

Google Hangouts

Google hangouts is Google's answer to video chat. You can chat one to one with someone or have a group chat.

You can call anyone on a tablet, ChromeBook, laptop, phone or pc that has Google hangouts and a webcam on the device. You can also send instant messages, photographs and videos.

To start the Google hangouts, open Google Chrome and navigate to:

`hangouts.google.com`

When hangouts opens up, you'll see a list of contacts you've been in contact with listed down the left hand side.

If you use hangouts a lot, you'll find all your most recent contacts listed here. Click on the names to see the conversations you've had with these contacts.

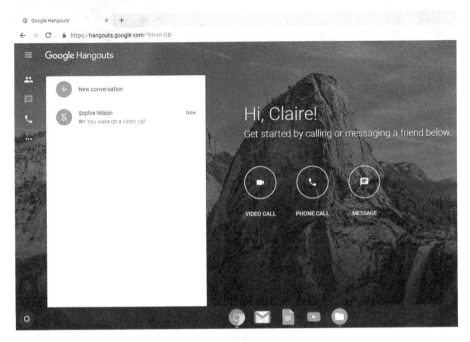

In the middle of the screen, you'll see three buttons. Here you can make a video call, a phone call, or send an instant message.

Messaging New Contacts

To contact someone new, click 'new conversation' on the top left of your screen.

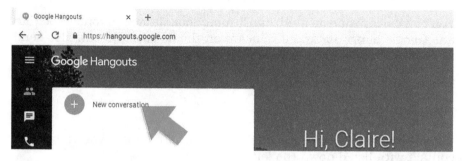

Type the person's name in the field, then select from the contact list that appears.

You'll see an instant message window pop up on the right hand side of your screen. Here, you can send instant text messages, as well as start video and audio chats. Just type your message in using the field at the bottom of the window.

Calling Someone New

To place a new video call, click the video icon in the middle of the screen.

Enter the name or GMail address of the person you're calling. Click the correct name from the drop down list.

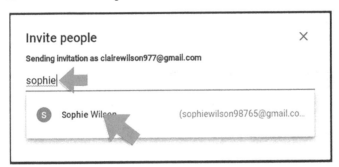

Click 'invite'.

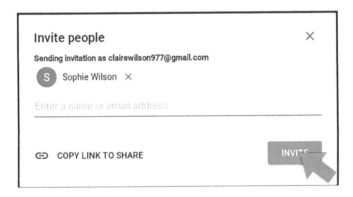

The other person will get a prompt on their hangouts window.

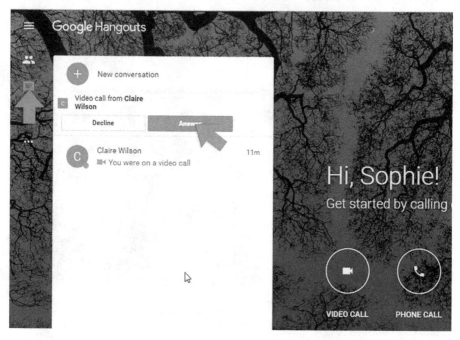

Now you can have a video conversation with that person.

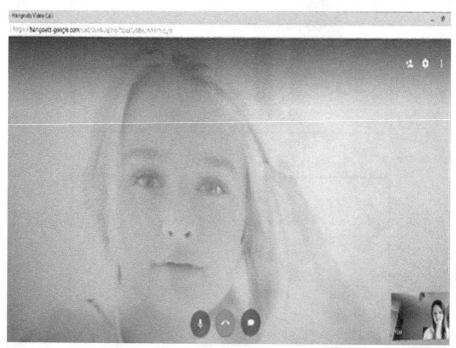

Calling Someone in Conversation Window

If you've had a conversation with someone before, you'll see their name listed in the recent contacts list when you open hangouts. Click on one of these names to see the conversations you've had.

This will open up your conversation window with that person. To place a video call, click the small camera icon on the top left.

When you place the call, you'll see an image of your webcam in the main viewer while you are waiting for the other person to answer.

The other person will get a prompt allowing them to either answer or decline the call.

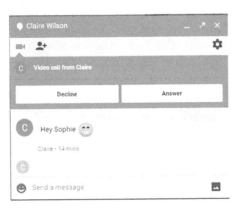

To answer, just select 'answer' from the prompt.

When the other person answers, you'll see their webcam in your main viewer. You'll also see a preview of your own camera on the bottom right of your screen, as you can see below.

Along the bottom of your screen, you'll also see three buttons. These usually disappear during a call - just click the screen to bring them up.

The button on the far left mutes your microphone so the person you're talking to can't hear you. Similarly the icon on the far right turns off your camera. Useful if you want a moment's privacy.

The red button in the middle closes your video call.

This is useful for keeping in touch with friends and family all over the world.

These calls are also free to make and you can chat as long as you like - you'll still have to pay for your internet connection though, whether that is through cable, broadband, wifi or cellular depending on your service provider.

Sending Images

You can send files such as photos using the conversation window.

To send an image, click the image icon on the bottom right of the conversation window.

Select 'upload photos'. Then click 'select a photo from your computer'.

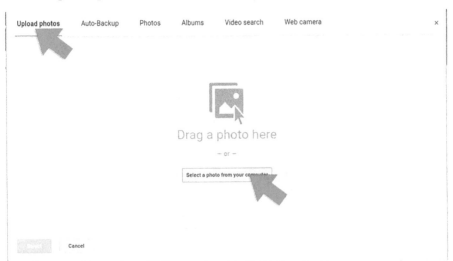

You can also send photos from Google Photos, albums, video search on the web, or the webcam on your ChromeBook.

Chapter 5: Web, Email & Communication

Select 'Google Drive', or 'My Files', depending on where the image you want to upload is stored.

Click 'open', when you're done.

You'll see a preview of the image in the conversation window. Click the 'send' icon in the middle of the image to send.

Sending Emoticons

You can send smilies and all sorts of other emotes in the conversation window.

To do this, click the smiley face icon on the bottom left hand side of the window.

Select a category of emoticons or stickers using the row of icons along the top.

Then click an emoticon or sticker from the list, to send or insert into your message.

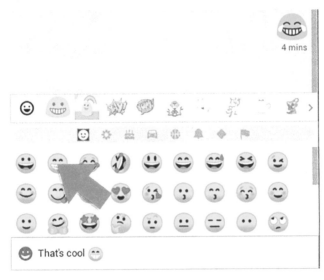

Chapter 6

Entertainment

Your ChromeBook has a large collection of multimedia apps available. You'll find these apps on your app launcher, and many more can be downloaded from the play store.

In this section we'll take a look at taking photos with your camera app, downloading apps, ebooks, movies, tv programmes and listening to music.

Google Play Store

Google Play allows you to search for and download digital media such as music, books, movies, and television programs, as well as apps and games.

You'll find the play store on your app launcher. Click the app launcher icon on the bottom left, then click the arrow in the top middle to open it up fully.

Click the play store icon to start the app.

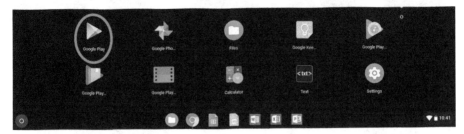

The play store will open in Google Chrome.

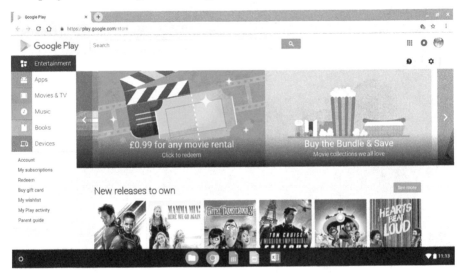

Play Music

Using the play music app you can purchase individual tracks and albums from the play store, or you can stream any music you like if you subscribe to 'play music'.

Click the app launcher icon on the bottom left, then click the arrow in the top middle to open it up fully.

Click the 'play music' icon.

Google play music will open in Google Chrome.

Downloading Music

To download tracks and albums, you'll need to go to the Google Play Store.

Open the Google Play Store from your app launcher, and select 'music' from the selections listed down the left hand side

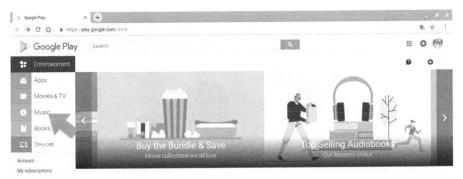

From here, you can browse through the latest releases and best selling tracks and albums. You can also use the search field at the top of the screen to find the songs, artists, or albums you want. Press enter on your keyboard to execute the search.

Browse through the search results and click the album or track you want.

Chapter 6: Entertainment

At the top of the screen, you'll see a write up of the album. Click the price tag to purchase and download the entire album.

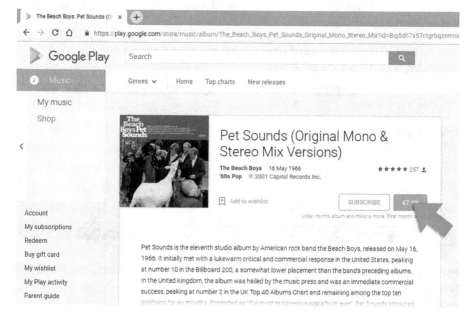

If you just want an individual track, scroll down the page and you'll come across a track list. This is a list of all the available tracks on the album.

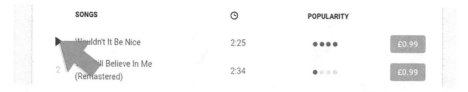

Hover your mouse pointer over the track number on the left hand side, and click the play icon that appears to hear a sample of the track.

	SONGS	⏱	POPULARITY	
1	Wouldn't It Be Nice	2:25	●●●●	£0.99
2	You Still Believe In Me (Remastered)	2:34	● ○ ○ ○	£0.99
3	That's Not Me (Remastered)	2:30	● ○ ○ ○	£0.99

Click the price tag on the right to purchase and download the track.

You'll find the track/album in the Google Play Music App.

Streaming Music

You can subscribe to Google Play Music family plan for a monthly fee and have access to millions of tracks and albums available. You can sign up for an individual account, which allows one person to access the Google Music Library, or you can select the family plan and allow up to 6 people to access the Google Music Library at a time from their own devices.

To sign up, select the Google Play Music app from your launcher.

Click the hamburger icon on the top left hand side of your screen to reveal the menus.

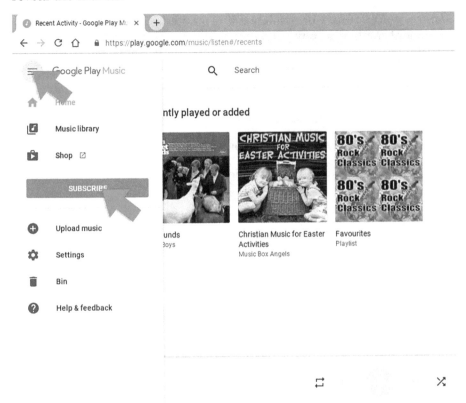

Select 'subscribe'.

Chapter 6: Entertainment

For individual plans select 'individual'.

Confirm your country of residence if prompted. Click 'add card' to add a payment method to pay your monthly subscription fee.

Select your payment method. You can use a credit/debit card or paypal.

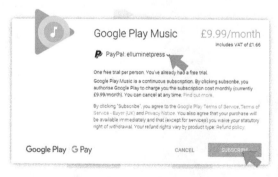

For family plans, select 'family' from the subscription options.

Family plan

Millions of songs at your fingertips, ad-free

£9.99/month   £14.99/month
                             Up to 6 people

INDIVIDUAL   **FAMILY**

Click 'upgrade now'.

Benefits   Family Library

Up to 6 family members   Your family also gets
can enjoy millions of   Family Library, for sharing
songs   purchased apps, games,
                  books and movies
Just £14.99/month

UPGRADE NOW

Click 'continue'.

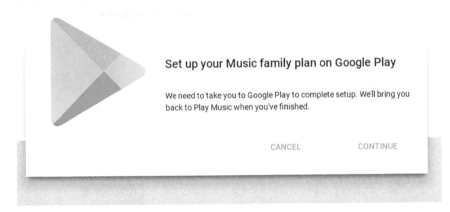

Set up your Music family plan on Google Play

We need to take you to Google Play to complete setup. We'll bring you
back to Play Music when you've finished.

CANCEL   CONTINUE

Click 'continue' again.

luminescentmedia

Family manager

Bring your family together on Google

To sign up for the family plan, first create a family group. As the family
manager, you must be 18 or older. Your family will see your email address and
profile photo.
Learn More

CONTINUE

Set up your payment method for family purchases. This is the card
that is charged if someone in your family group purchases an app,
book, or film. You'll receive a prompt on your account allowing you to
approve or deny the purchase. Enter the card details in the fields.

Set up a family payment method

You get an email whenever a family member buys something using this
payment method. You can approve each purchase made by 13 - 17 year olds.
Learn More

Add credit or debit card

Card number

\# | _____ VISA   MM / YY   CVC

ACCEPT

Scroll down and click 'accept' at the bottom of the screen.

Click 'continue' to set up Google Music Family Plan

Subscribe to the Google Play Music family plan

Next, you'll subscribe to the family plan

CONTINUE

Select your family payment method if you need to, then click 'subscribe'.

Now invite your family members to your family group. To do this enter their email addresses in the field at the top, or select their names from your contact list.

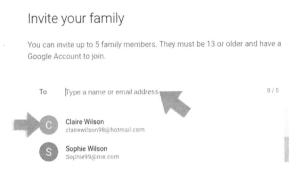

You can also invite family members from **families.google.com** *if you've already set up your family group.*

When the person checks their email, they'll find an email from Google Play in their inbox. Open the email and click 'accept invitation'.

Chapter 6: Entertainment

Click 'get started' and run through the setup wizard.

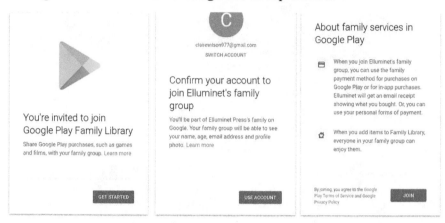

Select 'continue'...

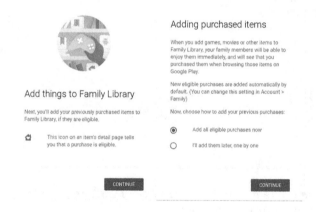

Now do this for each person you invited to your family group.

Searching for Music

If you have a subscription to the Google Play Music library, you'll see lists and recommendations on your Google Play Music home page.

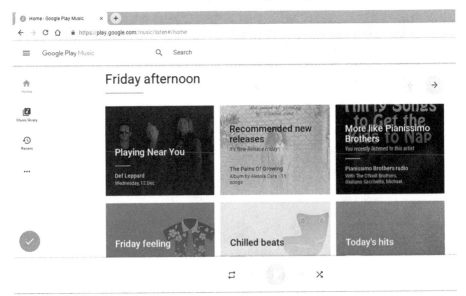

You can scroll down and browse through these recommendations. Just click on any of the thumbnails to view more details or to play the music.

You can also search for your favourite albums, artists, or tracks. To do this, type into the search field at the top of the home screen.

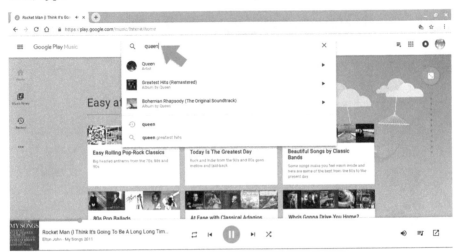

Chapter 6: Entertainment

From the search results, select an album or track...

Double click a track to play.

To add to a playlist, right click on the track and select 'add to playlist', then click the playlist you want to add it to, or click 'new playlist' to create a new list. If you're creating a new playlist, type in the name of the list...

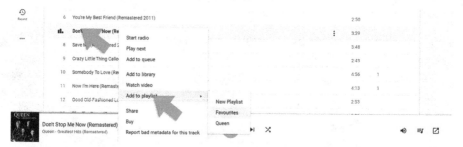

You'll find your playlists in your 'music library'.

Casting Music

If you have a ChromeCast device, you can 'cast' music to your TV or other ChromeCast enabled speakers.

When playing a track, you'll see the ChromeCast icon on the play bar.

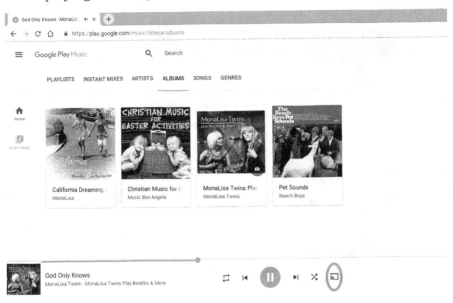

Select the device you want to cast to from the list.

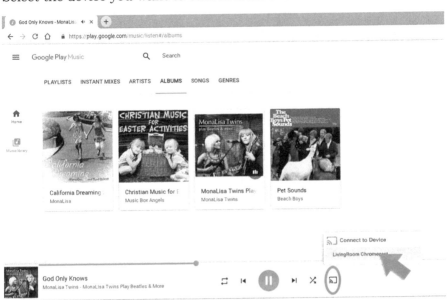

Play Books

With the books app you can buy and read ebooks in a wide variety of different genres from the play store.

Click the app launcher icon on the bottom left, then click the arrow in the top middle to open it up fully.

Click the Google play books icon.

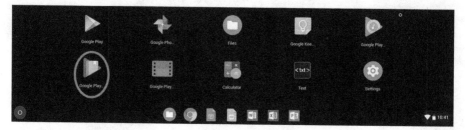

Google play books will open in Google Chrome.

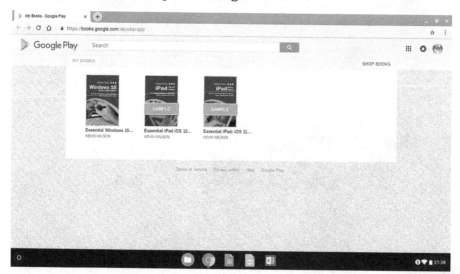

Here you'll see any books you have downloaded. Click the thumbnail book cover to open.

Downloading eBooks

To download new eBooks, you'll need to go to the Google Play Store. Open the Google Play Store from your app launcher, and select 'books' from the selections listed down the left hand side.

From here, you can browse through the latest releases and best selling books in various genres. You can also use the search field at the top of the screen to find book titles or authors you want. Press enter on your keyboard to execute the search.

Browse through the search results, click 'see more' on the top right to see all the results. Click on a book cover thumbnail to view details of the book.

Chapter 6: Entertainment

From here you'll be able to read a write up of the book, see reviews and other technical information. Click 'free sample' to read a sample of the book, or click the price tag, to buy and download the book.

Select your payment method if needed, then click 'buy ebook' to confirm.

You'll find the ebooks you download in the Google Play Books app on your app launcher. Click on one to open it up.

Play Movies & TV

Using the play movies app you can purchase or rent movies from the play store.

Click the app launcher icon on the bottom left, then click the arrow in the top middle to open it up fully.

Click the Google play music & TV icon.

Google play movies & TV app will open.

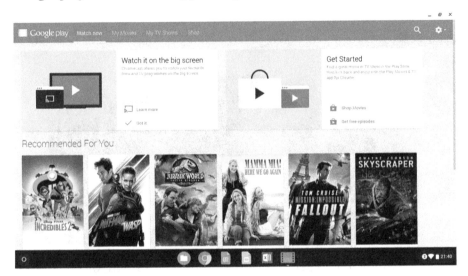

Here you'll see any movies or tv programmes you have downloaded, as well as the latest movies and tv shows for you to buy.

Chapter 6: Entertainment

Browsing the Store

To new movies, you'll need to go to the Google Play Store. Open the Google Play Store from your app launcher, and select 'movies & TV' from the selections listed down the left hand side.

You can also click 'shop' on the panel along the top of the TV & Movies app.

On the movies & TV home page, you'll see latest releases and top selling movies.

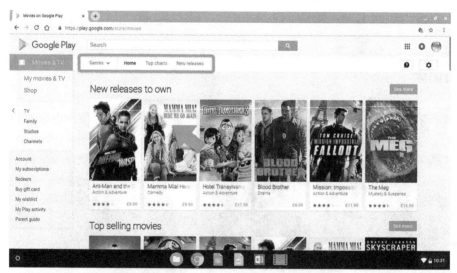

Along the top, you can select a genre to browse through, or see movies in that are in the charts, and new releases. Just click on the thumbnail cover to see details of the movies.

Searching for Movies

From the movies & TV section of the Google Play store, you can search for your favourite movies, actors, and genres using the search field at the top of the screen.

In the search results you'll see movies matching the search you entered. Click on one of the thumbnail covers to view details.

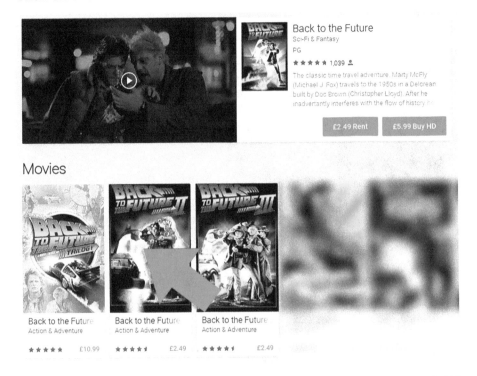

Chapter 6: Entertainment

Here, you'll be able to read a write up of the movie, read reviews, see casts lists, and watch trailers.

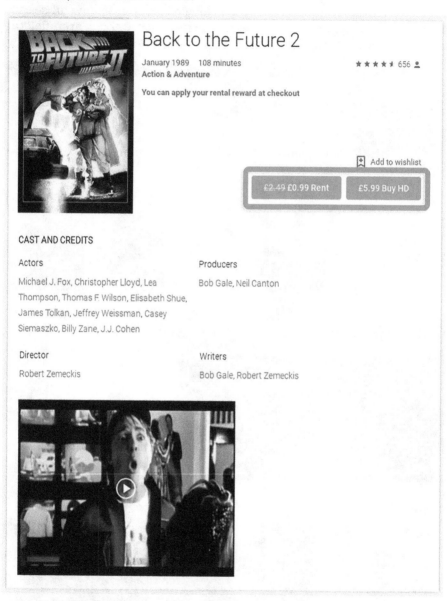

To buy the movie, click the 'buy' price tag. Some movies are available for rent. This allows you to download for 48 hours.

Select the quality you want. I'd select HD whenever possible, this gives you the best quality for watching your movie.

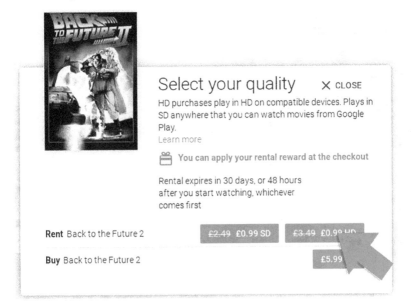

Select your payment method if you need to, then click 'rent', or 'buy' on the bottom right.

You'll find your downloaded movies & TV programmes in the Play Movies & TV app.

Chapter 6: Entertainment

Watching Movies

Open the Play Movies & TV app from your app launcher.

Click 'my movies' on the red panel at the top of the screen.

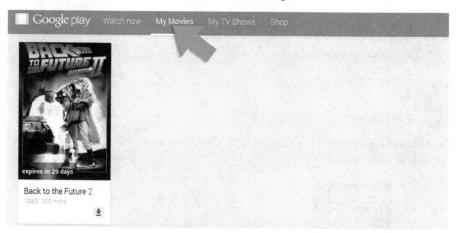

Click the thumbnail cover of the movie you want to watch.

On the movie details page, click play to start your movie.

Click on the full screen icon, sit back and enjoy your movie.

You can also cast your film to a TV or Projector, or you can connect to it using an HDMI cable, and watch your movie on a big screen.

Chapter 6: Entertainment

Searching for TV Shows

From the movies & TV section of the Google Play store, you can search for your TV shows, actors, and genres using the search field at the top of the screen.

From the Google Play store, select 'movies & TV' from the list on the left hand side, then select 'tv'.

Type your search into the field at the top of the screen.

From the search results select 'see episodes'.

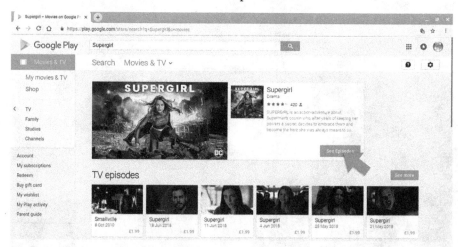

Select an episode to download and watch.

Projectors & TVs

You can hook your ChromeBook up to a digital projector or television. You can also cast your video wirelessly to a ChromeCast device plugged into your TV or projector.

HDMI

Your ChromeBook has an HDMI port on the side that will enable you to connect to a TV or projector. Most modern TVs & projectors will have at least 1 HDMI port on the back.

You can buy an HDMI cable from most electronic stores and online. An HDMI cable looks like the one below.

Plug one end into an HDMI port on your TV or projector, then plug the other end into the HDMI port on your ChromeBook.

ChromeCast

To use ChromeCast, first you'll need to buy a ChromeCast device, and plug it into an HDMI port on your TV or projector.

With ChromeCast you can stream from Netflix and YouTube, as well as any movie, TV show, or app from the Google Play Store. You can also use it to stream anything from Chrome browser on your ChromeBook.

Both your ChromeCast device and your ChromeBook will need to be on the same wifi network for it to work.

To cast a video you've downloaded from the Google Play store, open the Google Play Movies & TV app.

Select 'my movies' from the red bar along the top of the screen, then click on the movie you want to watch.

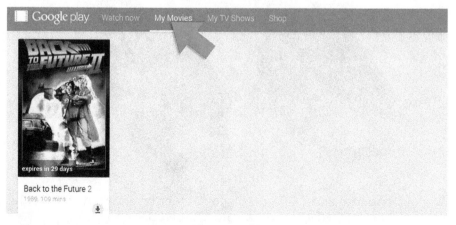

Click 'play' on the summary screen.

As you hover your mouse over the video, you'll see some icons. Tap the 'cast' icon on the top right hand side of the screen, then select your Chromecast device from the device list.

You can do the same for any movie or TV show you have downloaded from the Google Play Store.

The cast icon will only appear if your Chromecast device is plugged in, powered on, and connected to the same wifi network as your Chromebook.

Google Photos

With the photos app you can manage, store and enhance the photographs you take with your camera. You can also share photos on social media, or send them to friends and family.

Click the app launcher icon on the bottom left, then click the arrow in the top middle to open it up fully.

Click the Google photos icon.

Google Photos will open in Google Chrome.

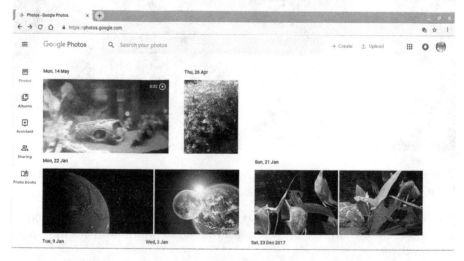

Viewing Photos

To view all the photos in Google Photos, click the photos icon on the left hand side.

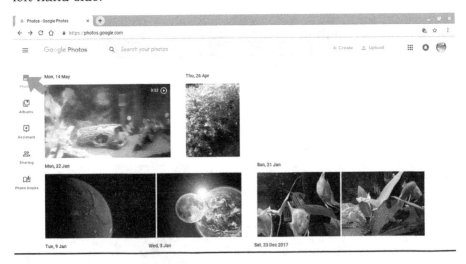

Scroll up and down, you'll see your photos listed in reverse chronological order. Click on one of the thumbnails to view the image in full.

To view albums select 'albums' from the list on the left hand side of your screen.

Along the top, you'll see albums, animations, movies, and things Google has created for you automatically, and any albums, collages or animations you have created yourself.

Adjusting Photos

To adjust a photo, select it from the photos section or album. The photo will open up. Click the adjustments icon on the top right.

You'll see a panel on the right hand side of the screen. The panel is divided into three sections: filters, lighting adjustments, and crop/rotate.

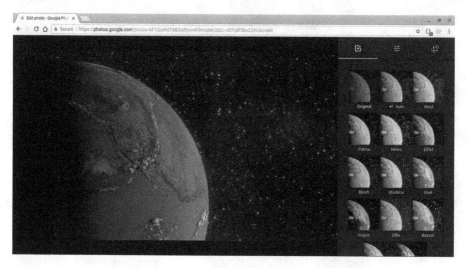

To make adjustments to the lighting, contrast, or colour, click the centre icon on the top middle of the panel on the right hand side of the screen.

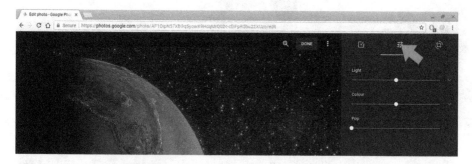

To change the general lighting and colour settings, move the 'light' and 'colour' sliders. To make the image pop off the page, use the 'pop' slider - try it see what happens.

126

To make more detailed changes to the lighting and contrast, click the small arrow next to the 'light' slider to open up the options.

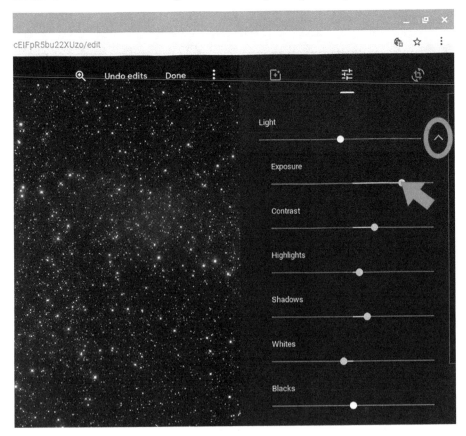

Use the individual sliders to adjust the different parts of the image. So...

- Exposure, lightens and darkens the whole image.

- Contrast is the difference between the dark and light parts of the image. Increasing the contrast can make parts of your image stand out.

- Highlights and whites, lighten and darken just the bright parts of the image. Eg you could darken the sky in a photo if it's too bright.

- Shadows and blacks, lighten and darken just the dark parts of the image. Eg you could lighten up the shadows of a photo.

When you're done, click the arrow next to the 'light' slider to close the lighting options.

127

Now, to adjust the colour, click the small arrow next to the 'colour' slider to open the colour options.

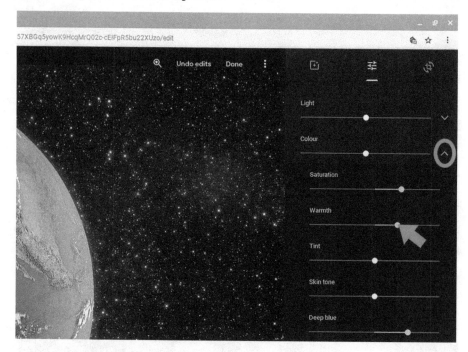

Saturation adjusts the intensity of the colours. For example, if you turn up the saturation, the colours become darker and more intense.

Warmth adjusts the colour cast of the image. If you increase the 'warmth' the photo becomes more orange, and if you decrease the warmth, the photo becomes more blue. This is useful if your photographs have come out too orange or too blue. If you photo is too orange (ie too warm), just turn the 'warm' slider towards the left.

Tint adjusts how much white is added to the photo

Skin tone enhances 'skin colours' in the photograph. This can help make people look a bit more natural in the photo.

Deep blue, is useful for oceans, skies, and anything that is blue.

Click 'done' on the top of the screen, when you're finished. Then click the arrow on the top left to return to your photos.

Crop & Rotate Photos

To crop a photo, click on it in the photos section. Then click the adjustments icon on the top right.

Select the icon on the top right of the panel on the right hand side of the photo.

You'll see the photo open up in a grid. On each corner of the grid, you'll see a resize handle. To crop the image, click and drag these handles around the part of the image you want to keep.

Click 'done' to accept the changes.

Chapter 6: Entertainment

To rotate an image, use the slider on the right hand side. Click where it says 0° then drag up or down until the image is level.

You can also rotate the image 90° counter clockwise using the icon on the top right.

To crop to an aspect ratio of the image, eg 16:8 or 4:3, click the aspect ratio icon on the top right.

Click 'done' on the top of the screen, when you're finished. Click the arrow on the left to return to your photos.

Creating Albums

Select the photos you want to add to your album.

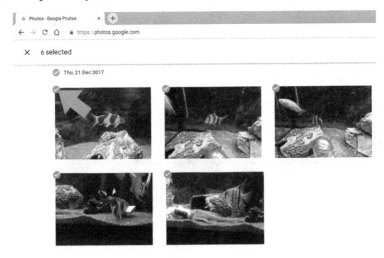

From the panel across the top of the screen, click the 'create' icon on the right hand side.

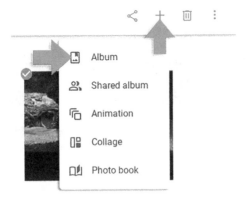

Click 'new album' to create a new album.

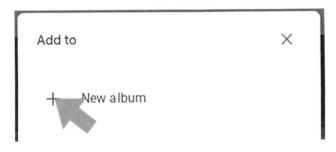

Give your album a name, then click the blue 'tick' icon on the top left of the screen.

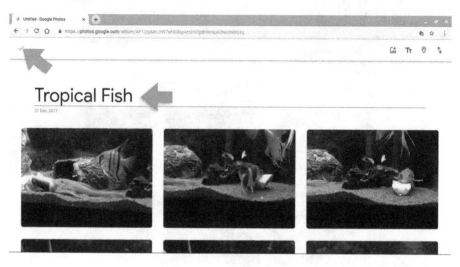

You'll find all your albums in your 'album' section of Google Photos. Select 'albums' from the panel on the left hand side of the screen.

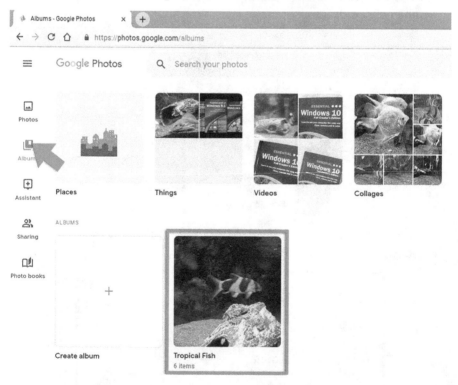

Collages

A photo collage is a composition made up of various different photographs assembled together. These are useful for posting to social media. To create a collage, select the photos you want to use from an album or the photos section. Choose six good ones.

Click the 'create' icon on the top right of the screen. From the drop down menu select 'collage'.

Click the adjustments icon to add a filter, or adjust the colour and brightness.

Click the share icon at the top to post your collage to social media, or send to a friend using email.

You'll find all collages you have created in your albums section.

Sharing Photos

Select the photo(s) you want to share from the photos section in Google Photos.

Click the 'share' icon on the top right of the screen.

Select the people you want to share the photos with.

Type in a message if you want to, then click the send icon.

When the other people check their email, they'll receive a message inviting them to view the photographs you shared.

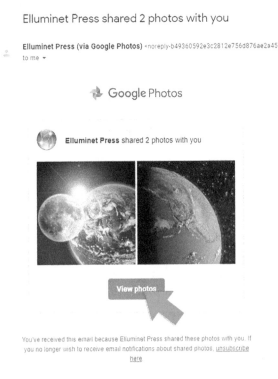

Click 'view photos' to open them up in Google Photos.

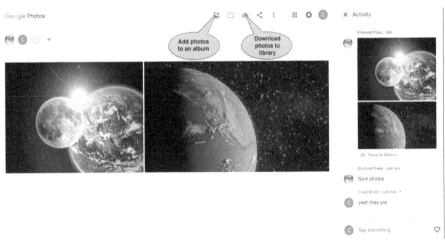

The person you shared your photos with can download them to their library, as well as add comments, and re share them with other people.

Sharing Albums

You can share an album on social media such as facebook or via email. To do this, select 'albums' from the icons on the left hand side of the screen.

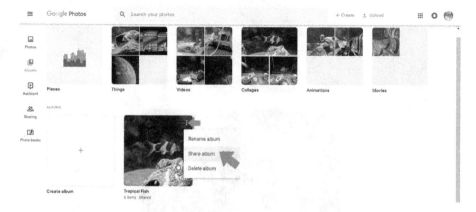

Click the three dots icon on the top of an album, then select 'share album' from the drop down menu.

Select the people or person you want to share your album with from your contact list, or enter their email address.

Click the blue send icon on the top right. This will send an email invitation with a link to your album.

136

You can also post directly to facebook. To do this, instead of selecting the people or person you want to share with, click the 'facebook' icon on the bottom of the share dialog box.

Follow the prompts to sign into facebook and post your album on your facebook timeline.

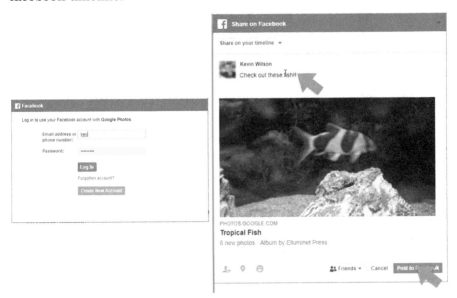

Sign into your facebook account if prompted, then in the 'share on facebook' popup, add a message to your post at the top, then click 'post to facebook'

Google Docs

Google Docs is an online word processor much like Microsoft Word, and is included as part of a free, web-based office suite developed by Google for its Google Drive service.

Getting Around Google Docs

You'll find Google Docs on your app launcher. Just click the icon to start the app.

When Google Docs opens, you'll see the documents you have been working on recently. You can click any of these to re-open them. To create a new document, click the red + on the bottom right of the screen.

We'll start with a blank document. Click the red + on the bottom right.

Chapter 7: Google Docs

Google Docs will open the main window where you can create your document.

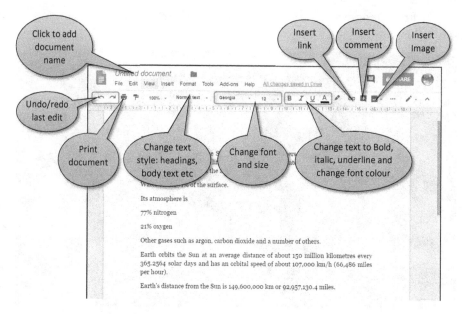

Along the top you'll see the document name. It's a good idea to rename this to something more meaningful that 'untitled document'. Click on the text and type in a name.

Underneath are the menus. This is where you'll find tools that are not represented as icons on the toolbar.

Under the menus you'll see the toolbar. This is where you'll find most of the tools you'll need to create and format your documents.

Using Paragraph Styles

Google Docs has several paragraph styles that are useful for keeping your formatting consistent.

For example you can set a font style, size and colour for a heading or title style...

Headings

To set the styles for a heading or paragraph, just highlight it with your mouse and click the drop down box 'normal text'.

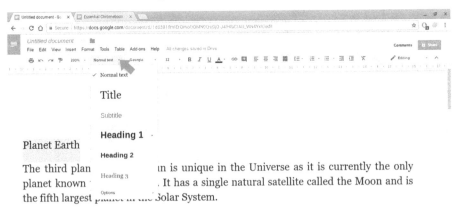

Bold, Italic, Underlined

To make text **bold**, *italic,* or underlined, highlight the text with your mouse and select the bold, italic, or underline icon from the toolbar.

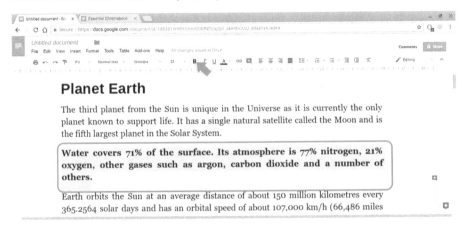

Changing Fonts

Google Docs has a variety of fonts to choose from. To apply a different font to your text, highlight the text, then click the font style drop down box as shown below.

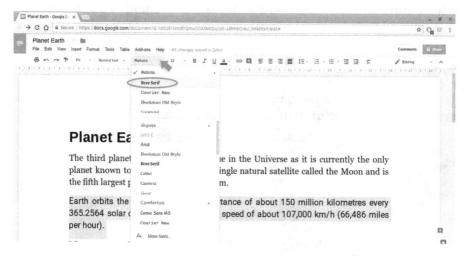

Font Colour

To change the colour of the text, first highlight it with your mouse. In the example below, I want to change the text colour of the second paragraph. To do this, click before the word 'Earth' and drag across the paragraph, to the end after '...miles per hour', to highlight it.

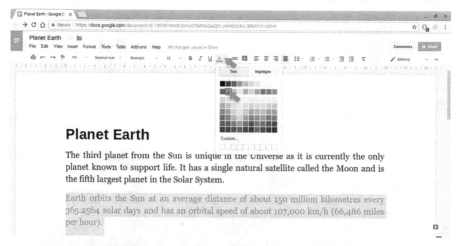

From the toolbar, select the font colour icon and from the drop down choose a colour. In this example I'm using red.

Justify Text

You can align text to different margins: left align, centred, right align, and fully justified.

> The third planet from the Sun is unique in the Universe as it is currently the only planet known to support life. It has a single natural satellite called the Moon and is the fifth largest planet in the Solar System.
>
> The third planet from the Sun is unique in the Universe as it is currently the only planet known to support life. It has a single natural satellite called the Moon and is the fifth largest planet in the Solar System.
>
> The third planet from the Sun is unique in the Universe as it is currently the only planet known to support life. It has a single natural satellite called the Moon and is the fifth largest planet in the Solar System.
>
> The third planet from the Sun is unique in the Universe as it is currently the only planet known to support life. It has a single natural satellite called the Moon and is the fifth largest planet in the Solar System.

In this example, I want right justify the first paragraph. This means the text is aligned to the right hand margin. To do this, click before the word 'The' and drag across the paragraph, to the end after '...solar system as shown above to highlight it.

> The third planet from the Sun is unique in the Universe as it is currently the only planet known to support life. It has a single natural satellite called the Moon and is the fifth largest planet in the Solar System.

Select the right align icon from the toolbar.

The selected text will move to the right hand margin.

> The third planet from the Sun is unique in the Universe as it is currently the only planet known to support life. It has a single natural satellite called the Moon and is the fifth largest planet in the Solar System.

Bullets Lists

Select the text using your mouse as shown below.

> Its atmosphere is
>
> 77% nitrogen,
> 21% oxygen,
> other gases such as argon, carbon dioxide and a number of others.
>
> Earth orbits the Sun at an average distance of about 150 million kilometres every 365.2564 solar days and has an orbital speed of about 107,000 km/h (66,486 miles per hour).

Then from the toolbar, click the bullet points icon on the right hand side.

You can also have different styles of bullets such as ticks, stars and so on. To get the drop down menu, click the small down arrow next to the bullet icon.

Bullet points will be added to the selected text.

> Its atmosphere is
>
> - 77% nitrogen,
> - 21% oxygen,
> - other gases such as argon, carbon dioxide and a number of others.

Numbered Lists

Select the text using your mouse as shown below.

> Its atmosphere is
>
> 77% nitrogen,
> 21% oxygen,
> other gases such as argon, carbon dioxide and a number of others.
>
> Earth orbits the Sun at an average distance of about 150 million kilometres every 365.2564 solar days and has an orbital speed of about 107,000 km/h (66,486 miles per hour).

Then from the toolbar, click the numbered points icon on the right hand side.

You can also have different styles of numbers such as roman numerals, letters, and so on. To get the drop down menu, click the small down arrow next to the numbered icon.

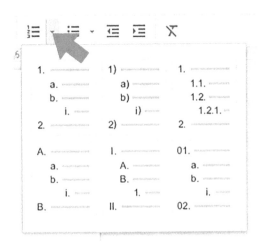

Numbers will be added to the selected text.

> Its atmosphere is
>
> 1. 77% nitrogen
> 2. 21% oxygen
> 3. Other gases such as argon, carbon dioxide, and a number of others.

Cut, Copy & Paste

To ease editing documents, you can use copy, cut, and paste to move paragraphs or pictures around on different parts of your document.

First select the paragraph you want to cut or copy with your mouse. I'm going to cut the last paragraph in the document below.

Click before the word 'Earth', and dragging your mouse across the line towards the end of the line, as shown below.

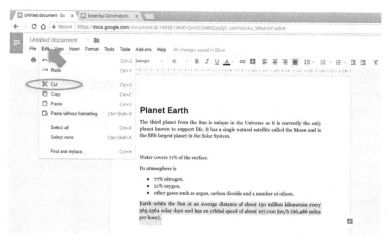

From the edit menu, select 'cut'. Now click on the position in the document you want the paragraph you just cut out to be inserted.

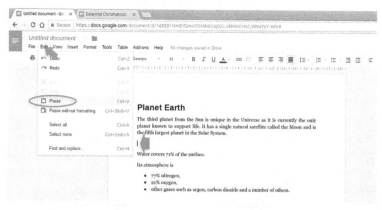

Once you have done that, click the 'edit' menu and select 'paste'.

If you wanted to copy something ie make a duplicate of the text, then use the same procedure except select 'copy' instead of 'cut' from the edit menu.

Adding Images

You can insert images from your Chromebook, from the web, Google Drive, your Photos App or directly from the onboard camera.

From your Chromebook

Click on the line in your document where you want your photograph or image to appear.

Go to your insert menu and click on 'image'. From the slideout menu select 'upload from computer'.

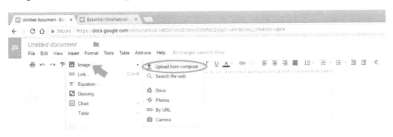

Choose the picture or photo you want on your Google Drive, from the dialog box that appears.

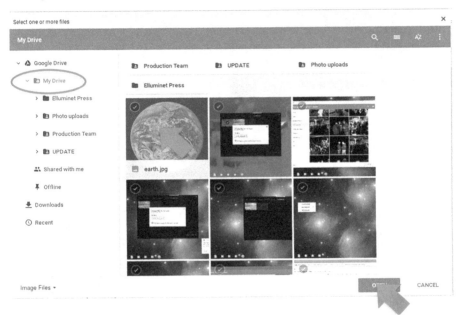

Click 'open' to insert the image.

From the web

You can add images from a Google Image search. To do this, click the 'insert' menu, then select 'image'. From the slideout select 'search the web'.

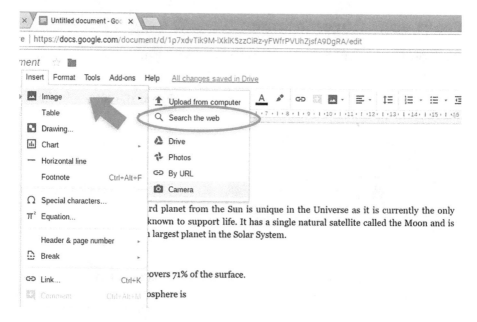

You'll see a search box appear on the right hand side of the screen. Type in the name of what you're searching for. In this example I need an image of the earth, so I'm going to type in 'planet earth'.

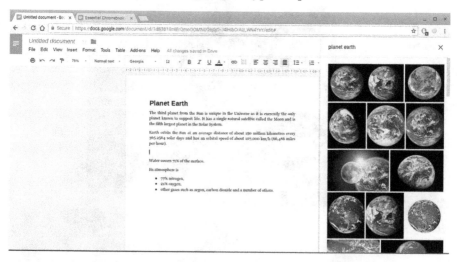

Click on one of the images to insert it into your document.

From your Photos

You can add images from your Google Photos App. To do this, click the 'insert' menu, then select 'image'. From the slideout select 'photos'.

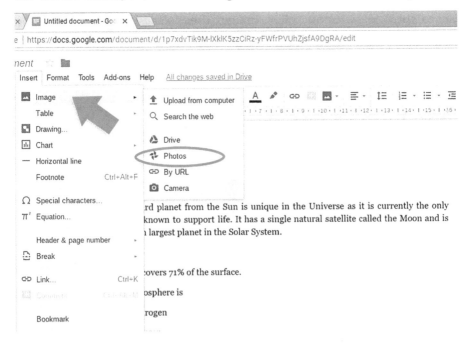

You'll see the Google Photos Panel appear on the right hand side of the screen.

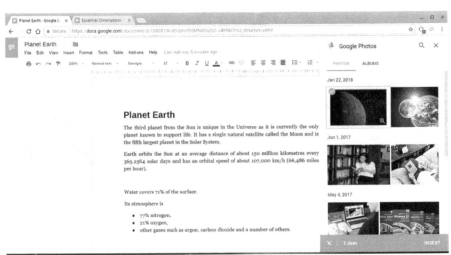

Browse through the photos and select the one you want to insert.

From your Camera

Probably works better on an android tablet, but can still be achieved using the onboard camera that comes with your Chromebook.

Go to the insert menu, click image, then select 'camera' from the slideout.

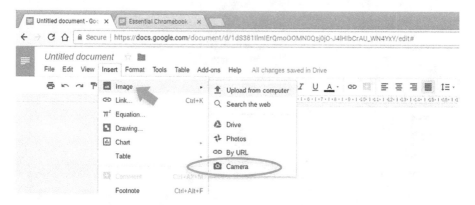

Click the yellow camera icon to take the photo.

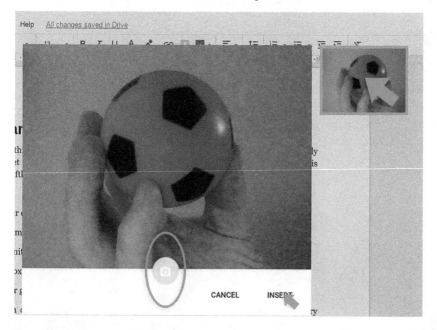

If you took more than one photo, select the one you want from the small thumbnails on the right.

Click 'insert' to add the image to your document.

150

Formatting Images

Right click on your image and select 'image options' from the popup menu.

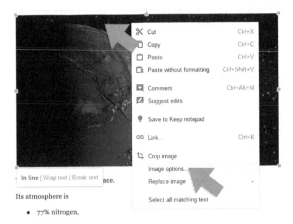

On the right hand side of the screen, you'll see the image options panel open up. From here you can recolour the image - that is give it a red, blue, green, or yellow hue, or turn it into black and white.

You can adjust the transparency of the image, as well as the brightness and contrast of the image using the sliders.

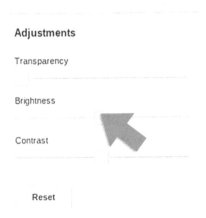

Cropping Images

To crop an image, right click on it and from the popup menu, select 'crop image'.

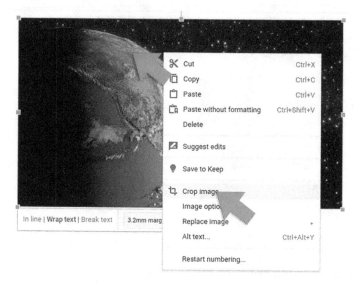

You'll see black crop handles appear on the corners and sides of the image. Click and drag these inwards, around the part of the image you want to keep as illustrated below.

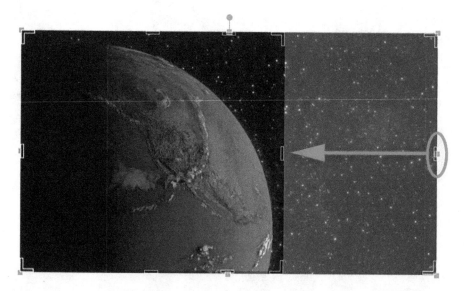

Click anywhere outside the image to execute the crop.

Adding Tables

First click the position in the document you want the table to appear.

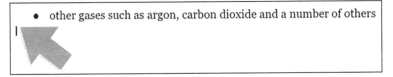

To add a table, click the 'table' menu and select 'insert table'. From the slideout, select how many rows and columns you want in your table.

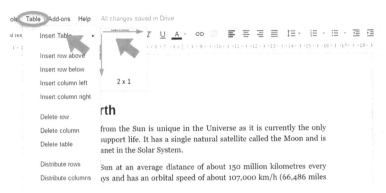

Inserting Rows & Columns

To insert a row or column, right click on the position in the table where you want to insert the row or column.

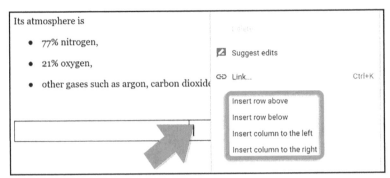

If you want to insert a row below the row selected, click 'insert row below'.

If you want to insert a column after the column selected, click 'insert column to the right'.

153

Saving Documents

Documents are automatically saved to your Google Drive. Make sure you give your document a name. You will see the document name on the top left of the screen. If you haven't given your document a name you'll see "untitled document" in the title.

Click on this title and type in a name for the document.

This will save it in Google Drive. To save in another folder on Google Drive, click 'my drive' then select the folder you want to save in.

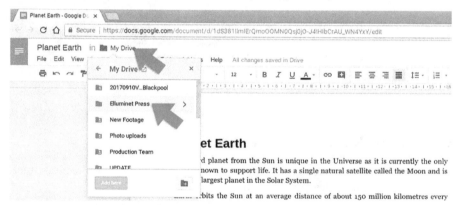

If you want to create a new folder, click the 'new folder' icon on the bottom right of the drop down.

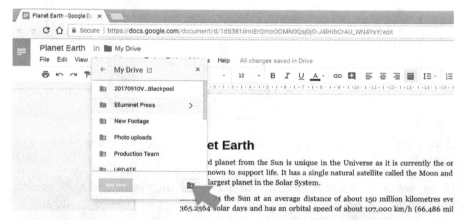

Opening Saved Documents

To open a document from Google Drive, double click on the document.

When you open Google Docs, you'll see a list of documents you've recently opened. Click on one of these to open it up.

To open a document within Google Docs, click the file menu, then select 'open'.

From the dialog box, select the file you want to open. Select 'my drive' to open a file saved on your Google Drive. Click 'shared with me' to open files other users have shared with you. Click 'recent' to open a file you've recently worked on.

You can also search for the file using the search field at the top of the screen.

Click on a file to select it, then click 'open'.

Printing Documents

To print a document from within Google Docs, click the file menu, then select 'print'.

From the dialog box, select the printer you want to print to. To do this click 'change', then select a destination.

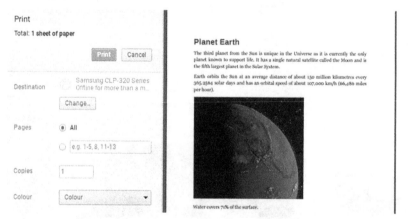

Enter which pages you want printed, or leave the option on 'all' if you want the whole document.

If you want the document in black and white, click 'colour', then change the setting to 'black and white'.

To print the document click 'print' at the top of the dialog box.

Sharing Documents

You can share your document using email and Google Drive's collaboration features.

To do this, click the 'share' icon on the top right of the screen.

Enter the names of the people you want to grant access to in the 'add more people' field.

Click the pencil icon to the right of the field and select 'can edit' if you want these people to be able to edit your document, if not select 'can view'.

Click 'send' when you're done.

If you just want a link to the document, click 'get shareable link'.

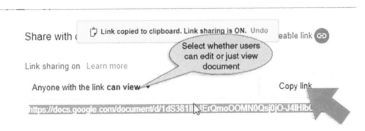

The link will be copied to your clipboard. From here you can paste into an email or another document.

Google Sheets

Google Sheets is an online spreadsheet programme much like Microsoft Google Sheets, and is included as part of a free, web-based office suite developed by Google for its Google Drive service.

What is a Spreadsheet

A spreadsheet is made up of cells each identified by a reference. The reference is made up by using the column, eg D, and the row, eg 10. So for a particular cell, you look to see what column it's in (D), then what row it's in (10). Put them together and you get the cell reference for that cell.

[COLUMN] [ROW]

So the highlighted cell in the illustration below would be D10.

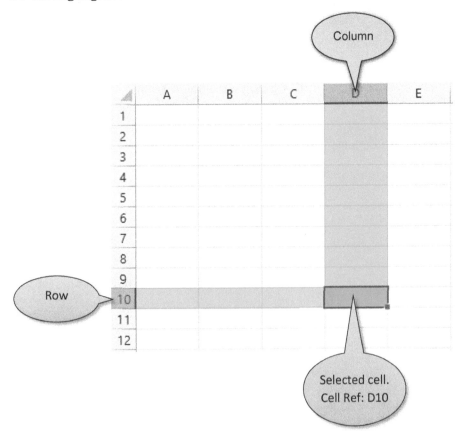

You can also select multiple cells at the same time. A group of cells is called as a cell range. You can refer to a cell range, using the cell reference of the first cell and the last cell in the range, separated by a colon.

[FIRST CELL in RANGE] : [LAST CELL in RANGE]

For example, this cell range would be A1:D10 (firstcell : lastcell).

Cell references are used when you start applying functions to the numbers in your cells.

In the example below, to add two numbers together, you can enter a formula into cell C1.

Instead of typing in **=5+5** you would enter **=A1+B1**.

The theory is, if you enter the cell reference instead of the actual number, you can perform calculations automatically and Google Sheets will recalculate all the numbers for you should you change anything.

For example, if I wanted to change it to **5+6**, I would just change the number in cell B1 without rewriting the formula in C1.

Now you can type any number in either cell A1 or B1 and it will add them up automatically.

This is a very basic example but forms the building blocks of a spreadsheet. You can use these concepts to build spreadsheets to analyse and manipulate data, as well as allow changes to the individual data and other parts of the spreadsheet without constantly changing formulas and functions.

Now that we understand the basics of what a spreadsheet is, lets take a look at Google Sheets.

Getting Around Google Sheets

You'll find Google Sheets on your app launcher. Just click the icon to start the app.

When Google Sheets opens, you'll see the spreadsheets you have been working on recently. You can click any of these to re-open them. To create a new spreadsheet, click the red + on the bottom right of the screen.

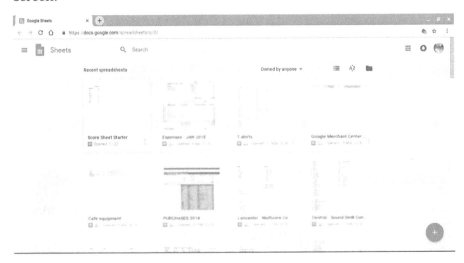

We'll start with a blank spreadsheet. Click the red + on the bottom right.

Chapter 8: Google Sheets

Google Sheets will open the main window where you can create your spreadsheet.

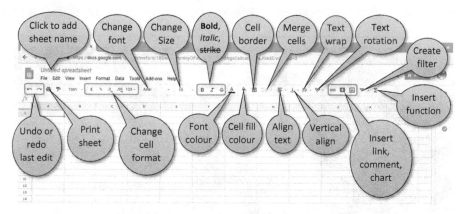

Along the top you'll see the spreadsheet name. It's a good idea to rename this to something more meaningful that 'untitled spreadsheet'. Click on the text and type in a name.

Underneath are the menus. This is where you'll find tools that are not represented as icons on the toolbar.

Under the menus you'll see the toolbar. This is where you'll find most of the tools you'll need to create and format your spreadsheets.

Then you have the formula bar *(fx)*. Here, you'll be able to see and add any functions or formulas in the selected cell.

Simple Text Formatting

In this example we are doing a basic scoring sheet. Enter the sample data into the spreadsheet as shown below.

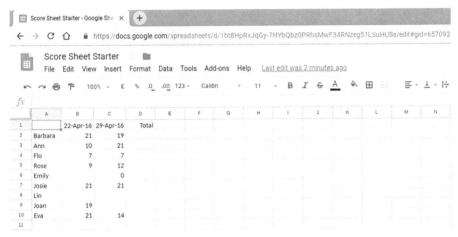

Bold, Italic, Strike & Underlined

Sometimes it improves the readability of your spreadsheet to format the data in the cells.

For example, we could make the column headings and the player's names bold.

First, select the cells you want to apply the formatting to, click the bold icon from the toolbar.

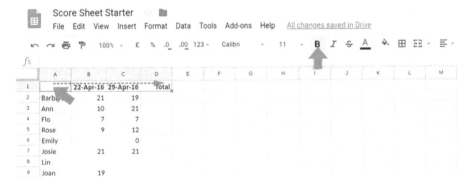

If you want *italic* text, click the 'I' icon on the toolbar. If you want ~~strike~~ text, click the 'S' icon. If you want <u>underlined</u> text, you'll need to go to the format menu and select 'underlined'.

Changing Fonts

First, select the cells you want to apply the formatting to.

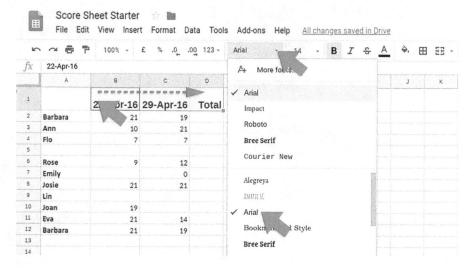

Click the font selector from the toolbar, and select a font from the drop down box.

Font Size

First, select the cells you want to apply the formatting to.

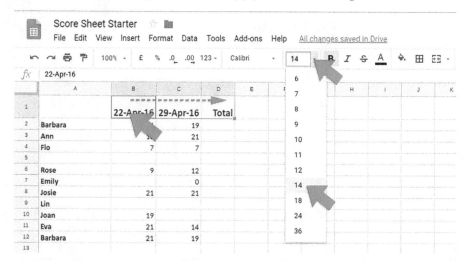

Click the font size selector from the toolbar, and select a size from the drop down box.

164

Cut, Copy & Paste

You can copy and paste a cell or cell range and paste it into another worksheet or in a different location on the same worksheet.

To perform a basic copy, select the cells you want to copy.

	A	B	C	D	E	F	G	H	I	J
1		22-Apr-16	29-Apr-16	Total						
2	Barbara	21	19							
3	Ann	10	21							
4	Flo	7	7							
5	Rose	9	12							

Right click on the selection, then select 'copy' from the popup menu.

	A	B	C	D	E	F	G	H	I	J
1		22-Apr-16	29-Apr-16	Total						
2	Barbara	21								
3	Ann	10	21	Cut			Ctrl+X			
4	Flo	7	7	Copy			Ctrl+C			
5	Rose	9	12	Paste			Ctrl+V			
6	Emily		0	Paste special			▸			
7	Josie	21	21							
8	Lin									

Right click the cell where you want the cells to be copied to. I'm going to paste the cells at the end of the table. From the popup menu, select 'paste'.

	A	B	C	D	E	F	G	H	I	J
1		22-Apr-16	29-Apr-16	Total						
2	Barbara	21	19							
3	Ann	10	21							
4	Flo	7	7							
5	Rose	9	12							
6	Emily		0							
7	Josie	21	21							
8	Lin									
9	Joan	19								
10	Eva	21	14							
11										
12		Cut			Ctrl+X					
13		Copy			Ctrl+C					
14		Paste			Ctrl+V					
15										
16		Paste spec			▸					
17										

Do the same for 'cut', except choose 'cut' from the menu instead of 'copy'.

Resizing Rows and Columns

You can resize a column or row by clicking and dragging the column or row divider lines as shown below.

You can also double click on these lines to automatically size the row or column to the data that is in the cell.

Inserting Rows & Columns

To insert a row between Flo and Rose, right click your mouse on the row 'Rose' is in. In this case row 5

Remember, Google Sheets always adds a row or column before the one you've selected.

Cell Alignment

This helps to align your data inside your cells and make it easier to read. You can align data in the cells to the left, center, or right of the cell.

To do this highlight the cells you want to apply the alignment to, then select the alignment icon on the toolbar. From the drop down box, click the centre icon to align everything to the centre of the cell, click the right hand icon to align everything to the right of the cell.

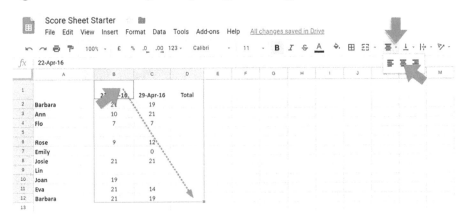

You can also align data vertically in the cell: top, middle, bottom. To do this highlight the cells you want to apply the alignment to, then select the vertical alignment icon on the toolbar.

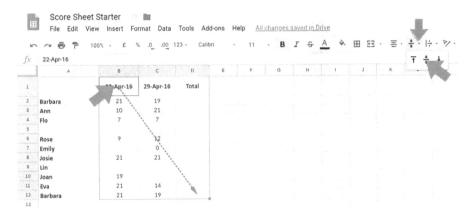

From the drop down box, click the left icon to align everything to the top of the cell, click the centre icon to align everything to the middle, and click the right hand icon to align everything to the bottom of the cell.

Cell Borders

To apply borders to your spreadsheet, with your mouse select the cells you want to format. In this case, I am going to do the whole table.

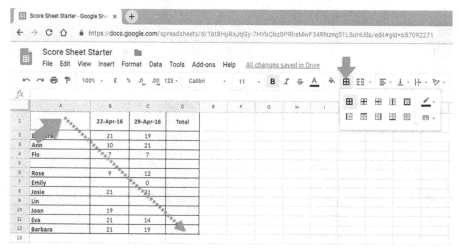

Select the borders icon from the toolbar. Lets take a look at the options on the borders drop down box.

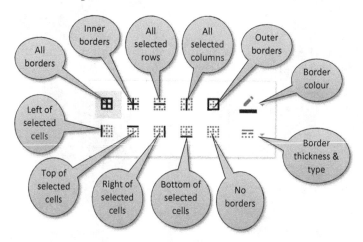

In the example, I want the borders around all the cells both inside and the outline. So from the dialog box click the 'all borders' icon.

To change the thickness, click the 'border thickness & style' icon and select an option.

To change the colour of the border, click the 'border colour' icon, and select a colour.

Using Formulas

If I wanted to add up all the scores in my score sheet, I could add another column called total and enter a formula to add up the scores for the two weeks the player has played.

To do this, I need to find the cell references for Barbara's scores.

Her scores are in row 2 and columns B and C circled below.

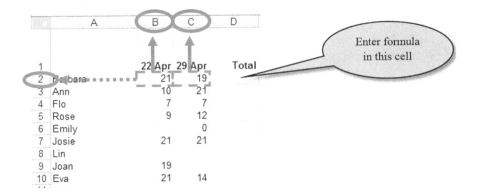

So the cell references are B2 for her score of 21, and C2 for her score of 19.

So we enter into the cell under the heading 'total'

    = B2+C2

Remember all formulas must start with an equals sign **(=)**.

To save you entering the formula for each row, you can replicate it instead.

If you click on the cell D2, where you entered the formula above, you will notice on the bottom right of the box, a small square handle.

I've enlarged the image so you can see it clearly.

Drag this handle down the rest of the column to replicate the formula.

Using Functions

A function is a pre-defined formula. Google Sheets has hundreds of different functions all designed to make analysing your data easier.

Count

Say I wanted to count the number of games played automatically. I could do this with a function.

Insert a new column after "29 Apr" into the spreadsheet and call it "Played". To do this, right click on the D column (the 'Total' column) and from the menu click 'insert column'.

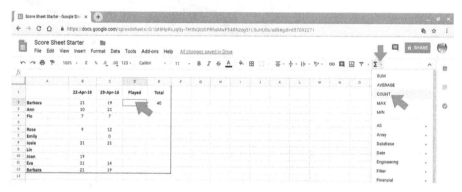

Make sure you have selected the cell you want the formula to appear in, then click 'insert function' icon on the toolbar.

Now, click and drag across the row of cells you want to apply the function to. In this example, I want to count the number of games a player has played, so I'd drag the selection box across the two scores in cells B2 to C2.

Press the enter key on your keyboard to execute the function. Drag the handle, down to replicate the formula down the column as normal, as shown in the previous example.

Auto Sum

Auto sum, as its name suggests, adds up all the values in a row or column.

To add up a row, click on the cell you want the total to appear in.

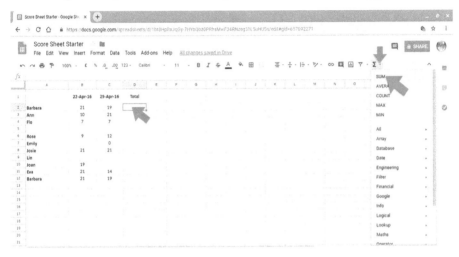

Now, click and drag across the row of cells you want to apply the function to. In this example, I want to add up the scores for each player, so I'd drag the selection box across the two scores in cells B2 to C2.

Press the enter key on your keyboard to execute the function. Drag the handle, down to replicate the formula down the column as normal, as shown in the previous example.

Types of Data

There are several different types of data you will come across while using Google Sheets. These data can be numeric such as whole numbers called integers (eg 10), numbers with decimal points (eg 29.93), currencies (eg £4.67 or $43.76), as well as date and time, text and so on.

Going back to our scoring spreadsheet, we need another column for the average scores. Insert a new column and type the heading 'Average' as shown below.

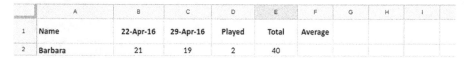

	A	B	C	D	E	F	G	H	I
1	Name	22-Apr-16	29-Apr-16	Played	Total	Average			
2	Barbara	21	19	2	40				

We are going to work out the average scores over the number of games the players have played. In the Cell F2 enter the formula

```
Average = Total Score / Total number of Games Played
```

The total score is in E2 and the total number of games played is in D2.

So we enter into F2:

```
= E2 / D2
```

Replicate the formula down the column as we did previously in the example.

Now we need to change the data type of the average to a number with two decimal places. To do this, select the values in the column, then click the data type icon from the toolbar.

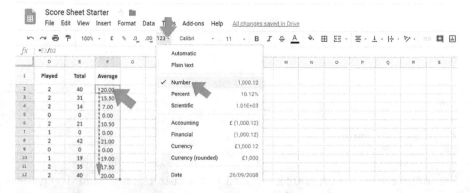

Select 'number' from the drop down menu.

It would be the same for recording the fees paid by the players. Insert another column and call it 'fee'. Say the fees are 4.50. When we enter 4.5 into the cell, Google Sheets thinks it's just a number, so we need to tell Google Sheets that it is currency.

Select all the data in the fee column. You don't need to include the heading row.

	B 22-Apr	C 29-Apr	D Played	E Total	F Average	G Fee
2	21	19	2	40	20.00	4.5
3	10	21	2	31	15.50	4.5
4	7	7	2	14	7.00	4.5
5	9	12	2	21	10.50	4.5
6		0	1	0	0.00	4.5
7	21	21	2	42	21.00	4.5
8			0	0	0.00	4.5
9	19		1	19	19.00	4.5
10	21	14	2	35	17.50	4.5

Click the data type icon on the toolbar.

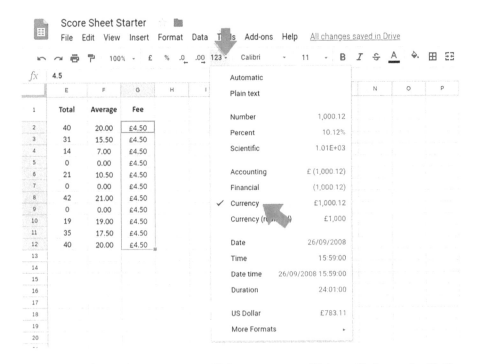

From the drop down menu click currency. This will format all the numbers as a currency.

173

Adding a Chart

There are many different types of charts to choose from, here are a few examples of some common ones.

First select all the names in the first column. This will be the X-Axis on the chart.

	A	B	C	D	E
1	Name	22-Apr-16	29-Apr-16	Total	
2	Barbara	21	19	40	
3	Ann	10	21	31	
4	Flo	7	7	14	
5				0	
6	Rose	9	12	21	
7	Emily		0	0	
8	Josie	21	21	42	
9	Lin			0	
10	Joan	19		19	
11	Eva	21	14	35	
12	Barbara	21	19	40	
13					

Now hold down the control key (ctrl) on your keyboard. This allows you to multi-select. While holding down control, select the data in the total column with your mouse. This will be the Y-Axis on the chart. Note the data in the names column is still highlighted.

Click the chart icon on the toolbar.

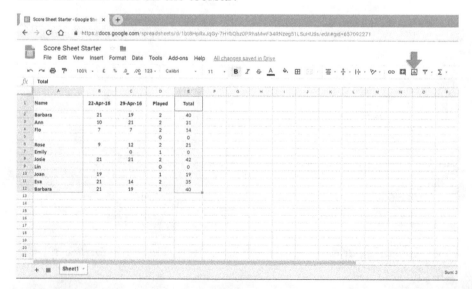

From the chart editor that appears on the right hand side, select the chart type you want. You can change it to a line chart, bar chart, column chart, pie chart, and so on.

To edit the char title. Click the title on the chart and type in a name. On the chart editor on the right hand side, you can change font, size, and alignment using the controls.

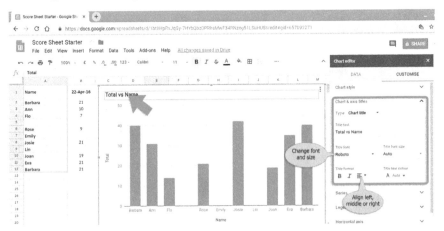

To change the x and y axis labels. Click the label on the chart.

In the chart editor that appears on the right hand side, click 'title text' and type in a label.

Chapter 9

Google Slides

Google Slides is an online presentation programme much like Microsoft PowerPoint or Apple Keynote, and is included as part of a free, web-based office suite developed by Google for its Google Drive service.

You can also connect your ChromeBook to a projector or TV screen to give your presentation.

Getting Around Google Slides

You'll find Google Slides on your app launcher. Just click the icon to start the app.

When Google Slides opens, you'll see the presentations you have been working on recently. You can click any of these to re-open them. To create a new presentation, click the red + on the bottom right of the screen.

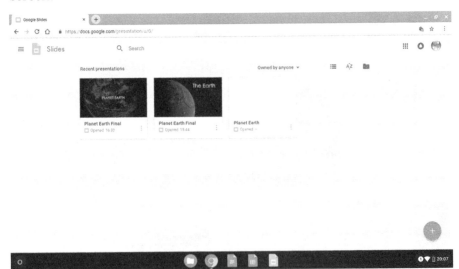

We'll start with a blank presentation. Click the red + on the bottom right.

Chapter 9: Google Slides

Google Slides will open the main window where you can create your presentation.

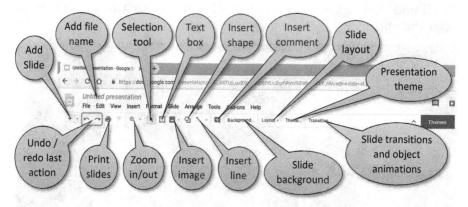

Along the top you'll see the presentation name. It's a good idea to rename this to something more meaningful that 'untitled presentation'. Click on the text and type in a name.

Underneath are the menus. This is where you'll find tools that are not represented as icons on the toolbar.

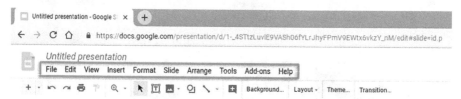

Under the menus you'll see the toolbar. This is where you'll find most of the tools you'll need to create and format your presentations.

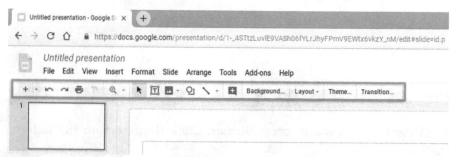

Designing a Slide

Lets begin by adding the title to our first slide. First, select a theme from the templates on the right hand themes panel. Once you have selected a theme, click the white cross on the top left of the panel to close it.

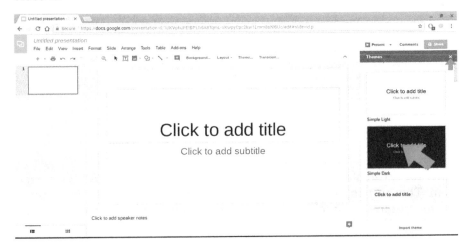

On your slide, click where it says 'click to add title'. This is a place holder for you to enter a title.

Enter the title 'Planet Earth'.

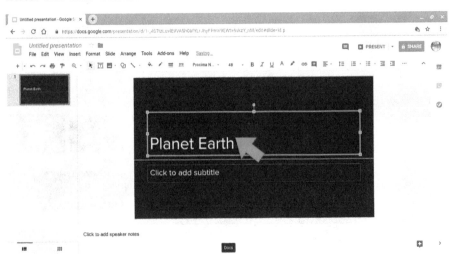

In this example, we won't be adding a subtitle, but you can add one if you want to.

Lets add some images to spice our title slide up a bit.

Add an Image

To add an image, select the slide you want to add the image to using the slide selector on the left hand side. Go to the insert menu then select 'image'.

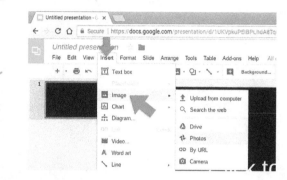

Now, from the slideout menu, select where you are adding the image from. This can be uploaded from your computer, the web, Google Drive, Google Photos, a direct weblink, or from your on-board camera.

From Photos

To add an image from Google Photos, select 'photos' from the image slideout menu. Google Photos contains photos you've taken with your android phone, or any other tablet you've signed into with your Google Account.

Google Photos will open in a panel on the right hand side, scroll through, click a photo then click 'insert'.

From the Web

To add an image from the web, select 'the web' from the image slideout menu. Google Search will open up in the panel on the right hand side. Type in your search into the field at the top

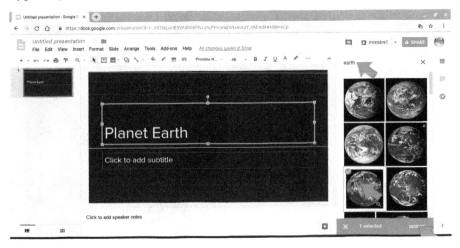

Click on the image you want then click 'insert'.

From your Google Drive

To add an image from your Google Drive, select 'Drive' from the image slideout menu. In the panel on the right hand side click 'my drive'. Any images stored on your Google Drive will open up in the panel on the left hand side.

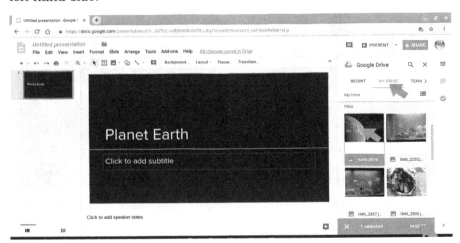

Click on the image you want then click 'insert'.

Resize an Image

When you click on an image on your slide, you'll see some resize handles appear around each corner.

Click and drag these resize handles to resize the image.

You may need to move the image into position. To do this, click and drag the image into position.

Crop an Image

Click on the image you want to crop, then from the toolbar, select the 'crop' icon.

You'll see some crop handles appear around each corner.

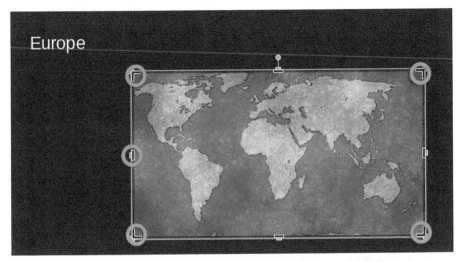

Click and drag these crop handles around the part of the image you want to keep. In this example, I only want to highlight Europe on this map.

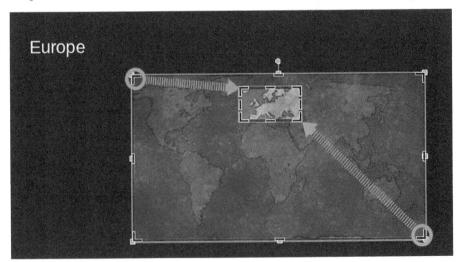

You may need to move the image into position. To do this, click and drag the image into position. Resize the image if needed.

183

Add a Video

You can add YouTube videos, or your own videos stored on Google Drive.

To do this, select the slide you want to add your video to, from the slide selector on the left hand side. From the insert menu, select 'video'.

From the dialog box that appears, select 'search' to search the web for a YouTube video, or click 'Google Drive' to use one of your own videos.

In the search field at the top of the screen, type in your search and press the enter key on your keyboard.

From the search results, select the video you want to insert, then click 'insert'.

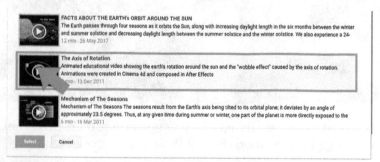

Videos on YouTube have a lot of rubbish in them that you don't need. You can trim the beginning and end of the video, so it starts and ends exactly in the right place. To do this, right click on the video on the slide. From the popup menu, select 'format options'.

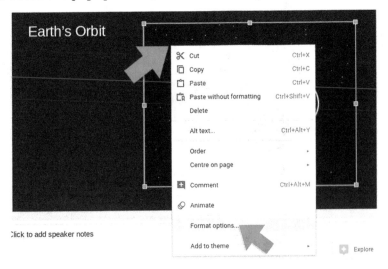

The 'format options' panel will open on the right hand side of the screen. From here hover your mouse over the video progress bar and you'll see a silent preview of the video. Click on the position you want the video to start.

Click 'use current time' to trim the start time to the position in the video. Repeat the procedure for the end times.

Slide Layer Arrangement

In the example below, I've added an image to the title slide.

You'll notice when you add an image, video, or other object, it covers the title or another object. This is because Google Slides constructs slides using layers. So the title "Planet Earth" will be on one layer, and the image will be on another layer.

Now, because the image was inserted after the title, the image layer is on top of the title layer. We want the title layer on top. We need to send the image to the back layer.

To do this, right click on the image or object, then from the popup menu, select 'order'. From the slideout, select 'send to back'.

This will put the image in the background. Now you can see the title, and you can drag it into position on the slide.

Add a New Slide

To continue building our presentation we need additional slides to show our information. To add a new slide, click the small down arrow next to the 'New Slide' icon.

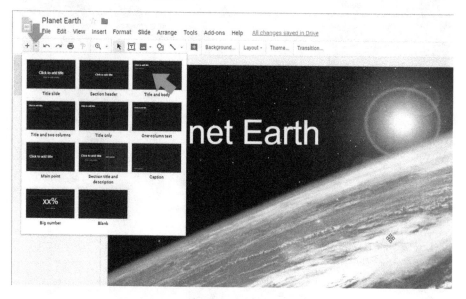

From the drop down menu, select 'title and body' because we want a title on the slide but also we want to add some information in bullet points.

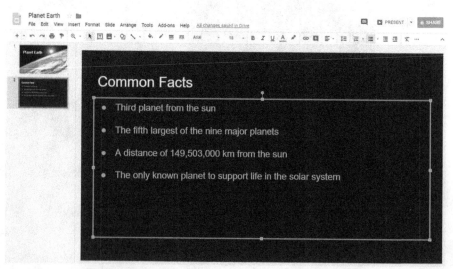

Now enter the data into your new slide.

Change Slide Layout

Select the slide you whose layout you want to change. Then go to the 'slide' menu and select 'apply layout'.

From the slideout menu, select a template from the options.

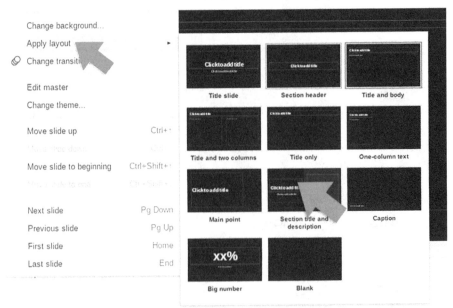

189

Slide Masters

Slide masters allow you to create layouts and templates that are common to all your slides, so you don't have to make those changes to each slide.

Say you are creating a presentation and want a company logo on the bottom, you can add it to your slide master and the logo will appear on every slide you create.

To edit your slide masters, go to the slide menu and click 'edit master'.

The larger slide listed down the left hand side is your master for all slides. The ones below are masters for individual slide templates such as 'title slides' or 'title and body' slides. These appear in the 'new slide' drop down menu. You can split them up so you can create templates for specific slides.

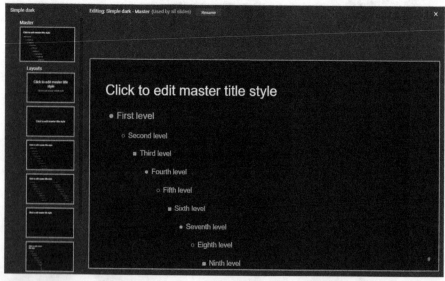

In this simple example, I am going to add the company logo to the bottom right of every slide. To do this, click on the larger master slide in the list on the left hand side.

Open your file explorer and navigate to your Google Drive folder, or the folder where the picture you want is saved. Click and drag your image onto the master slide.

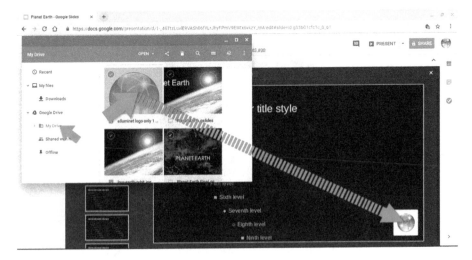

Notice, the logo we just added appears on all the slides.

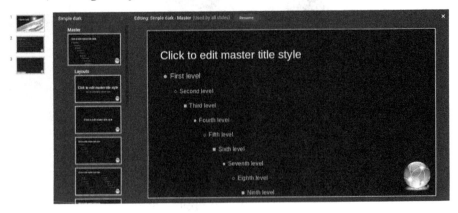

Click the small white x on the top right to close the masters.

Slide Transitions

A slide transition is an animation or effect that is displayed when you move from one slide to the next.

To add transitions to your slides, click the slide you want to add the transition to, then click 'transition'.

From the animations panel on the right hand side of the screen, you can select from several pre set transitions. If you click on a transition, for example 'fade', this will apply the transition to the selected slide.

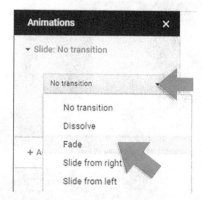

Select how fast you want the slides to transition, using the slider.

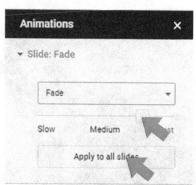

By default, the transition is only applied to the slide you have selected. Click 'apply to all slides' if you want to apply the same transition to all the slides you have added to your presentation

192

Slide Animations

You can add animations to slides to move text boxes, make bullet points appear, animate shapes and so on. This can help to make your presentation flow so objects and text appear at the right time while you're presenting. Animation effects can also help to emphasise certain points.

Effects

Looking at the slide below, say you wanted each bullet point to appear one at a time, instead of all at once.

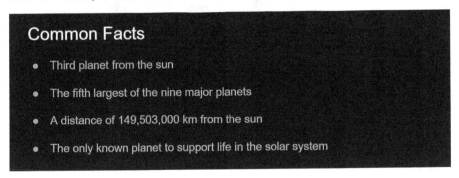

To add an animation effect to the bullet points, click 'transition' on the right hand side of the toolbar.

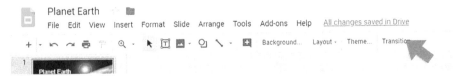

This will open up the 'animations' panel on the right hand side of your screen.

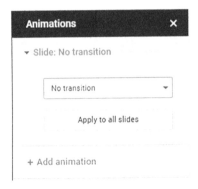

First, select the object you want to add an animation to. In this case the textbox with the bullet points in.

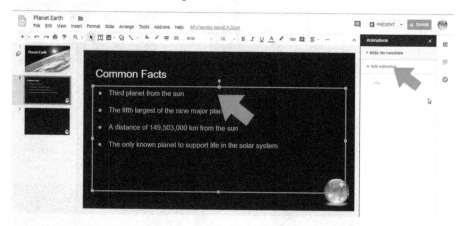

In the first drop down box, select the animation preset you want, eg 'fade in'.

In the second drop down box, select 'on click' - meaning you click the mouse to show the next point.

Select 'by paragraph'. This means a 'paragraph' will appear at a time. A new paragraph is created each time you press return when typing in your slide information into the text box.

Click 'play' to preview the animation.

Insert a Table

We are going to add a table to a new slide. In this example I have added a new slide with 'title only'.

To add a table to this slide, go to the 'insert' menu and select 'table'. From the slideout, select the number of columns and rows. This table is going to have 2 columns.

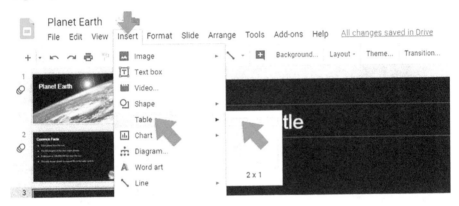

Your table will appear in the centre of the slide. You can type in your data.

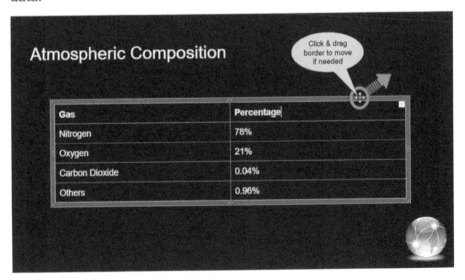

Press the tab key on your keyboard to insert a new row, when you get to the end.

Click & drag the solid double blue border to move the table into position on your slide.

Add a Chart

We are going to add a chart to a new slide. In this example I have added a new slide with 'title only'

Click the 'insert' menu, then select 'chart'. From the slideout, select the type of chart you want. In this example, I am going to use a nice pie chart.

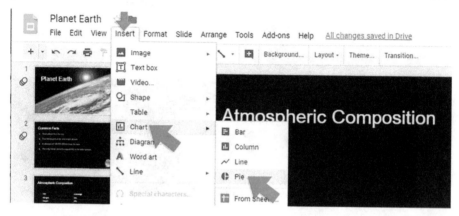

Google Slides will insert a default chart. To enter your own data, click the down arrow on the top right of the chart and select 'open source'.

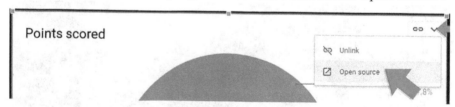

In the spreadsheet that opens, enter your data in the first two columns.

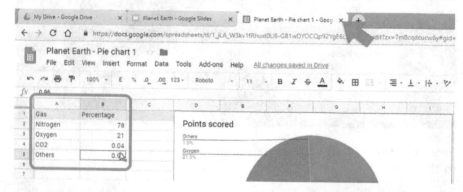

Click the x on the tab at the top of the screen to close and return to Google Slides.

Printing Presentations

To print your slides, click the 'file menu', then select 'print settings and preview.

Click '1 slide with notes' - the second icon along the toolbar at the top, then from the drop down menu, select how many slides you want on each page. For handouts to give to your audience, select 6 slides per page. This will print 6 small slides on each page, leaving them some room to take notes. Click 'print'.

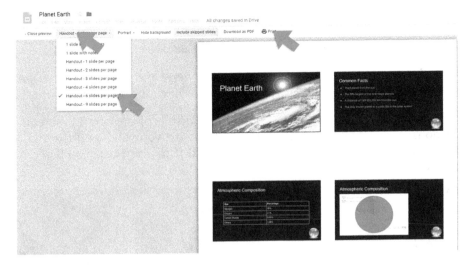

Select the printer you want to print to, and the number of copies you want.

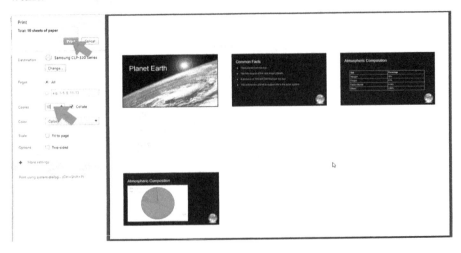

Click 'print' when you're done.

Giving your Presentation

First connect your ChromeBook to your projector or TV. When you do this your ChromeBook will extend its desktop onto the projector or TV. This enables you to have a presenter view on your ChromeBook screen with presenter notes, slide lists and other tools, while the audience see just the presentation.

Open your presentation, then click the small arrow next to 'present' on the toolbar on the right hand side.

Two windows will pop up, your presenter view, and your presentation view. You may need to drag your presenter view out the way.

Now, move your presentation view onto your projector or TV screen. To do this, click and drag the window tab with your slide, off the right hand side of the ChromeBook screen until it disappears. You'll see it appear on your projector or TV screen.

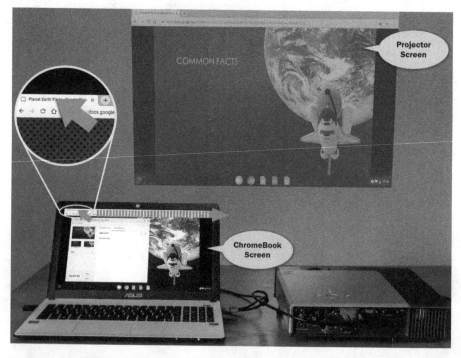

Some ChromeBooks you'll need to drag if off the left hand side of the screen - try this if it doesn't work.

On the projector or TV screen (move your mouse pointer to the right until it appears on the projector/tv screen), click the three dots icon on the top right, then click the 'full screen' icon.

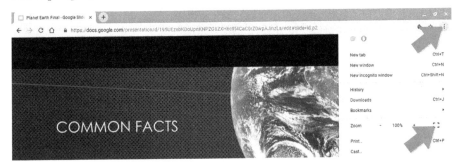

Now, maximise the presenter display on your ChromeBook screen.

You'll end up with something like this. You'll be able to control your Google Slides presentation using the presenter view on your ChromeBook.

Present with ChromeCast

To be able to cast your presentation to a ChromeCast device, your ChromeBook will need to be on the same Wi-Fi network as your ChromeCast device. The ChromeCast device can be plugged into a TV or a projector.

Open your Google Slides presentation, then click the small down arrow next to the 'present' icon. From the drop down menu, select 'present on another screen'. If it's greyed out, check your wifi settings on your ChromeCast device and ChromeBook.

From the popup box that appears, select your ChromeCast device. Your presentation will appear on your TV or projector screen.

Now that your ChromeBook is completely wireless, you can give your presentation.

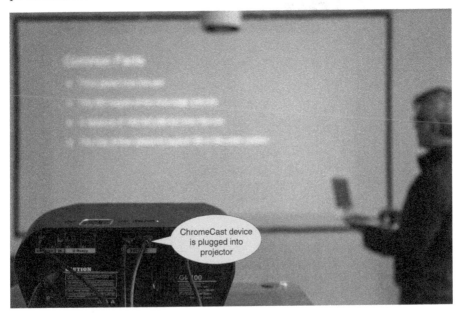

On your ChromeBook you can use a laser pointer, see your presenter notes, as well as advancing and selecting slides to show. You'll see a control bar popup when you move your mouse pointer to the bottom of the screen.

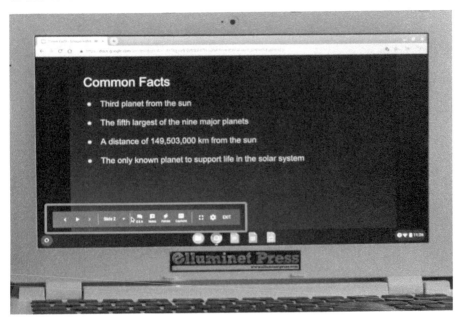

Index

Index

G

H

I

J

K

L

N

Index

CPSIA information can be obtained
at www.ICGtesting.com
Printed in the USA
BVHW091413241220
596436BV00003B/109